D0501280

PRAISE FOR
FUTURE FORWARD

Through his work at IDG, Patrick McGovern shaped the way that millions of people grew to understand the enormous potential of computers and how they would change the world. He was also known for being a caring and thoughtful boss—two traits that extended to his generous philanthropy.

—BILL GATES,
founder of Microsoft

Every great leader, from Benjamin Franklin to Steve Jobs, leaves behind a valuable set of lessons to be learned from their lives and careers. Pat McGovern was such a leader, and in this insightful book, Glenn Rifkin provides a dramatic, clear-eyed look at this visionary entrepreneur and the leadership lessons he used to build his global company. McGovern's wisdom about business and people puts him in the pantheon of the best and most successful leaders.

—WALTER ISAACSON,
bestselling author of *Steve Jobs,*
Benjamin Franklin, and *Leonardo da Vinci*

Glenn Rifkin has beautifully captured the Pat McGovern I knew and admired: curious, bold, innovative, and visionary. Pat was a true MIT original, with an iconic story of entrepreneurial success. *Future Forward* reminds us of Pat's extraordinary commitment to the McGovern Institute for Brain Research at MIT, an anchor for arguably the greatest concentration of brain science researchers on the planet. I am delighted that a wide audience will have this wonderful opportunity to read about Pat's impact—past, present, and future—on science and society.

—L. RAFAEL REIF,
president of MIT

Future Forward offers a vivid look at how Pat McGovern built a global organization able to innovate time and again. McGovern understood that innovation, at its best, is a team sport, and over the course of his extraordinary career, he propelled IDG's employees to build an agile and innovative organization. His successes and missteps provide invaluable lessons for leadership in a marketplace in which change and innovation are demanded.

—LINDA A. HILL,
professor and chair of the Leadership
Initiative at Harvard Business School

Pat McGovern is one of the unsung heroes of the tech business. His invisible hand helped many companies like Apple, Dell, and IBM. Read this book because it's about time that Pat's vision and wisdom see the light of day.

—GUY KAWASAKI,
chief evangelist for Canva and former
chief evangelist for Apple

Truly great companies are built on ephemeral but critical "soft" assets— culture, ethics, integrity, a deep-seated valuing of employees, and a genuine reverence for customers. This Pat McGovern playbook guides executives on how to build and leverage these powerful capabilities and keep them central to the life of all successful organizations.

—GEORGE F. COLONY,
founder and CEO of Forrester Research

Pat McGovern was a visionary leader who recognized early on the power and influence of information technology. McGovern's unique leadership philosophy created a remarkable company that spread the gospel of IT to every continent, and influenced countless managers and researchers around the world, including me. Glenn Rifkin has effectively captured McGovern's mission and the critical leadership lessons he taught his thousands of IDG employees. *Future Forward* is a must-read for aspiring leaders who want to harness the impact of the ongoing technology revolution.

—ERIK BRYNJOLFSSON,
professor at the MIT Sloan School of Management
and coauthor of *Machine Platform Crowd*

Pat McGovern was an entrepreneur's entrepreneur, by which I mean he grew his startup not merely by hiring experienced and energetic people, but by recruiting and supporting entrepreneurs. He tolerated corporate inefficiency to get entrepreneurial energy. And he loved people, especially customers, so he backed entrepreneurs who loved them, too.

—Bob Metcalfe,
professor of innovation at the University of Texas,
inventor of Ethernet, and founder of 3Com

Having known Pat McGovern for several decades, his influence and mentorship left an indelible mark on my career. *Future Forward* skillfully offers the set of leadership lessons that formed the basis for McGovern's remarkable success in building his company, IDG, into a global technology media giant. This is a provocative book which goes well beyond the usual prescriptive business offerings. Instead, Rifkin brings McGovern's lessons to life with detailed examples of his visionary outlook and his devotion to IDG's mission. Given the complexity of global business today, the timing couldn't be better for this invaluable set of lessons.

—Jim Breyer,
founder and CEO of Breyer Capital

Pat McGovern was one of the most important—and least famous—media moguls of the twentieth century. Glenn Rifkin gives you a chance to get to know him, and shares some of the key lessons from a business empire that stretched from Boston to Beijing.

—Scott Kirsner,
columnist at the *Boston Globe* and
cofounder of Innovation Leader

Glenn Rifkin has managed to capture Pat McGovern's spirit and his story—that of someone who came of age with the modern computing industry and understood from an early age how computing would transform the world.

—John Markoff,
former technology writer at the *New York Times*
and author of *Machines of Loving Grace*

FUTURE
FORWARD

FUTURE FORWARD

Leadership Lessons from **Patrick J. McGovern,** the Visionary Who **Circled the Globe** and Built a **Technology Media Empire**

GLENN RIFKIN

New York Chicago San Francisco Athens London Madrid
Mexico City Milan New Delhi Singapore Sydney Toronto

Copyright © 2019 by Patrick McGovern. All rights reserved. Printed in the United States of America. Except as permitted under the United States Copyright Act of 1976, no part of this publication may be reproduced or distributed in any form or by any means, or stored in a database or retrieval system, without the prior written permission of the publisher.

1 2 3 4 5 6 7 8 9   LCR   23 22 21 20 19 18

ISBN   978-1-260-14280-8
MHID   1-260-14280-9

e-ISBN   978-1-260-14281-5
e-MHID   1-260-14281-7

Library of Congress Cataloging-in-Publication Data

Names: Rifkin, Glenn, author.
Title: Future forward: leadership lessons from Patrick McGovern, the visionary who
    circled the globe and built a technology media empire / Glenn Rifkin.
Description: 1 Edition. | New York : McGraw-Hill Education, 2018.
Identifiers: LCCN 2018016817| ISBN 9781260142808 (hardback) | ISBN 1260142809
Subjects: LCSH: Leadership. | Management--Technological innovations. | McGovern,
    Patrick Joseph, 1937-2014. | BISAC: BUSINESS & ECONOMICS / Leadership.
Classification: LCC HD57.7 .R534 2018 | DDC 658.4/092--dc23 LC record available at
    https://lccn.loc.gov/2018016817

McGraw-Hill Education books are available at special quantity discounts to use as premiums and sales promotions or for use in corporate training programs. To contact a representative, please visit the Contact Us pages at www.mhprofessional.com.

*For my mom, Lillian, who continues
to inspire me every day.*

*For my dad, Sonny, who was gone far
too soon, but has never left my side.*

AUTHOR'S NOTE

Life is lived forward but understood backwards.
—Soren Kierkegaard

Pat McGovern's voice is distinctly present throughout this book. I was able to quote him extensively from interviews I conducted with him over several decades. There is also a trove of published articles and other media profiles and interviews, and IDG corporate communications, including a vital and lengthy video history interview done in 2000 by Daniel Morrow, then executive director of Computerworld Honors Program. Nearly all of the comments from others throughout the book are taken from interviews I personally conducted either specifically for this book or in earlier profiles I'd written about McGovern. Sources of other quotes can be found in the Bibliography in the back of the book.

CONTENTS

Patrick J. McGovern Jr.

FOREWORD

Marc Benioff,
founder and CEO of Salesforce

Pat McGovern was a true giant in the technology industry, a remarkable visionary who was near the center of every technology revolution over nearly half a century, from semiconductors and mainframes to the Internet and smartphones. He foresaw the incredible impact technology would have on society and across every industry. IDG, his company, created nearly 300 information technology publications, 460 websites with 280 million technology readers around the world, and event and research arms that chronicled and analyzed the story of this amazing digital transformation.

I grew up a passionate reader of his publications, including *PCWorld* and *Macworld*. I got my start in technology writing computer games for the Atari computer in high school and then working at Apple, writing programs for the infant Macintosh during summer breaks from college. When I actually met Pat during my tenure at Oracle, it was like meeting a childhood hero. He was generous with his time and advice, and incredibly knowledgeable about every facet of the industry. Every time I met with Pat he remembered the details from our previous conversation and then proceeded to ask me about every aspect of my life. His memory was legendary—each year he met every US-based employee in his company to give them a holiday bonus, and he remembered not only their names but specifics about their work and families.

My most momentous encounter with Pat occurred in the fall of 1999, just as I was starting Salesforce. We were both standing in line at a United Airlines gate waiting to board a flight from San

Francisco to Los Angeles. I shared my idea for creating a company that would make buying business software as easy as buying a book on Amazon. After hearing me out, Pat quickly volunteered to invest. From his deep experience and open mind, Pat immediately understood—unlike more than a dozen Silicon Valley venture capitalists I pitched who dismissed the idea for Salesforce—how the business world was about to undergo a seismic shift into the cloud. Pat became one of the first significant investors in my start-up. After his passing, his family told me that he had never sold the stock, which must have produced at least a 1,000 percent return!

Looking back on my 35-year career in the tech industry, I know that without mentors like Pat guiding me along every step of the way, I would not have been able to build Salesforce from an idea into a Fortune 500 company that forever changed the enterprise software industry. Today, young entrepreneurs often look to me, as I did to Pat, for insight into the future of technology and best practices for building a successful business. What I can share with them, among other things, are the leadership lessons I gleaned from Pat.

Pat was a true listener, a risk taker with an entrepreneur's mind that allowed him to see what others could not see. When China opened its doors to Western nations in 1979, Pat saw an opportunity to bring his flagship *Computerworld* publication to the communist country. He quickly formed a U.S.-China joint venture to publish *China Computerworld*, which had more than two million readers at its peak. IDG went on to launch 40 publications in China. He saw how entrepreneurs around the world were creating the future, and he had the foresight to create a global network of venture capital funds, which today have more than $3.6 billion under management.

But Pat didn't see technology or his business as isolated from his community and humanity. This was his unique gift—he served as an inspiring role model for me and other entrepreneurs looking for ways to give back to society. He viewed technology in terms of how it could make the world a better place and traveled throughout the world looking for insight and inspiration to feed this passion. He understood that a company's culture is its greatest asset, treated his employees, partners, and customers as part of a family, and made this real through his everyday interactions. He established corporate values to live by, such as showing respect for the dignity of each individual and striving for excellence in customer service.

Pat's philanthropic efforts were also exemplary. In 2000, with a $350 million gift from Pat and his wife, Lore, the McGovern Institute for Brain Research was established at MIT with a mission to understand how the brain works and to discover new ways to prevent or treat brain disorders. He didn't just donate money; he engaged with scientists, hosted tours, and inspired others, including me, to follow in his philanthropic footsteps. My wife, Lynne, and I have donated to build hospitals and bring in physicians and researchers who could have a major impact on improving the health of the children in our local communities of San Francisco and Oakland, and around the world.

While Pat is no longer with us, his influence is still felt. He was a gift to us all, a trailblazing visionary who showed an entire generation of entrepreneurs what it means to be a principles-based leader and how to lead with higher values.

INTRODUCTION

By Christmas of 1983, I had been working at *Computerworld* for nearly a full year. For a technology neophyte, this immersion into the exploding computer industry was astonishing. A revolution was underway as personal computers, networks, and powerful new software applications were fueling a shift in both the business and personal sides of this world. Computers were moving from glass-enclosed data centers to individual desktops, and the implications were enormous. Being at *Computerworld*, widely considered the bible of the technology information marketplace, was a fortuitous happenstance, a front-row perch from which to observe and meet the likes of Steve Jobs, Bill Gates, Larry Ellison, Thomas Watson Jr., Ken Olsen, Mitchell Kapor, and other industry heavyweights intent on changing the world.

This was before the advent of Apple's Macintosh, Microsoft's Windows, the Internet, smartphones, Wi-Fi, broadband, and the flood of technology-driven upheaval around the globe. But you could feel the earth moving, and there wasn't any doubt that something big was happening right at the tip of your keyboard. For journalists like me, whose careers were birthed when electric typewriters and Wite-Out were de facto tools of the trade, this new era was exhilarating.

Inside *Computerworld*, on a wintry afternoon a couple of weeks before the holidays, a buzz of a different kind was sweeping through the weekly newspaper's editorial offices in Framingham, Massachusetts. Word got out early in the day that Patrick J. McGovern, the formidable founder and CEO of our parent company, International Data Group (IDG), was going to be making his annual holiday rounds. Although the several hundred staff members in the building were adults, the feeling could only be described as giddy, a childlike sense of anticipation that reminded me of grade-school birthday parties.

I had seen McGovern in the building a few times during the year, but we had yet to meet, and he had already taken on the Paul Bunyanesque persona that turns ordinary businesspeople into celebrities. Larger than life, he was a big man who stood six feet, three inches tall and had the burly build of an NFL linebacker. He had a loud, distinctive voice and laugh that could be heard across a huge room. When we got word that Pat was in the building, work essentially ceased. We stayed at our desks in the cubicles that dotted the newsroom, feigned effort, but accomplished little as Santa in a dark blue suit and yellow tie approached. To be clear, our excitement was not only due to the wide-eyed exuberance of celebrity worship. There was the mercenary, Pavlovian vibe that emerged with the reality that Uncle Pat, as he was fondly called, had arrived with a Brinks truck loaded with some serious dough for each of us. He was here to hand out Christmas bonuses, and though the amount was meager compared to the six-figure bonanza bonuses of Wall Street investment bankers, it was a considerable sum for blue-collar journalists, production workers, and sales staff. That year, the bonus was equal to a month's pay, and that was a good reason to anticipate his arrival.

What made the event more memorable was the fact that McGovern, a media mogul by any measure, a wealthy, self-made visionary who transformed the technology information and research industry, handed out every envelope personally. He stopped at every desk, greeted every individual by name, shook hands, chatted about their work, their families, their dreams, and left behind a glow of good feeling that dwarfed the money and created an indelible imprint.

The fact that he did this with every employee in the company in every office in the United States was mind-boggling. By the time I joined, there were 13,000 employees around the globe and 5,000 in the United States alone. The scope of his effort, his determination to make that personal connection, spoke volumes about the man. For those of us who had worked at other companies, the idea of the CEO personally delivering a bonus and a good word was pure fantasy. If you were lucky, you got a cooked turkey, a Swiss Army knife, or a holiday memo from the chief to the troops. The odds that the CEO would personally deliver said turkey were very slim. But Pat McGovern was a different kind of executive, an iconoclast who was driven not merely by profit but by a desire to better the lives and careers of his employees and a lifelong calling to understand technology's impact on humanity. He was indeed on a mission.

When Pat McGovern started the company in 1964, not long out of MIT, he had a perfect combination for entrepreneurial success: an abundance of self-confidence, a prescient vision, and a wellspring of curiosity to find out what he didn't know and spread this information around the globe. In an era when computers were giant, mysterious, unattainable machines guarded by the high priests of the data center, McGovern foresaw an immense shift in the power of these machines to impact individuals, to enhance the human brain, and to spawn a better future.

That he operated in a familial manner and built an employee-friendly corporate culture just added to his reputation. In the 1980s, the era in which Gordon Gekko declared, "Greed is good," Pat McGovern chose to share the wealth. That's not to say he wasn't making a fortune for himself, because he was. He became a billionaire and was a regular on the *Forbes* list of the richest people. What he proved was that being good to his employees turned out to be a very sound business strategy.

If you were lucky enough to be part of the workforce near where IDG was headquartered in Massachusetts, the Christmas bonus was only the beginning. The company threw a lavish annual holiday party, hosted by McGovern and his wife, Lore Harp McGovern, in a ritzy downtown Boston hotel just before Christmas. Attendees brought their spouses and significant others, ate and drank and danced the night away, and some went home with door prizes of trips for two to tropical resorts, ski chalets, and Europe. Each year, McGovern and the executive team would create a holiday video to share the habitually positive corporate results and thank everyone for a job well done. Dressed as *Star Trek*'s Captain Kirk, Batman, Ben Franklin, Obi-Wan Kenobi, or James Bond, McGovern showed no reluctance to shed a little dignity for a good laugh.

News staffers went on an annual trip to resorts in the Bahamas or Puerto Rico for an "editorial meeting," and IDG was among the first companies in the country to take advantage of federal regulations allowing employee stock ownership programs. The ESOP created a cadre of millionaires among IDG's longest-serving employees and allowed others, such as me, to take a nice nest egg along with us when we left the company. Many who departed for jobs at rival organizations realized quickly that they'd made a mistake and returned to IDG.

What McGovern created was a large extended family. In a high-powered, often cutthroat industry like high tech, it was unusual to feel part of a culture of inclusion where your CEO had your back, valued your ideas, prodded everyone to push their own envelopes, and accepted failure as a stepping-stone to achievement.

As my tenure continued, I came to learn that McGovern's contributions far exceeded the corporate largesse. The empire he had built starting in 1964 played a major role in the evolution of computer technology around the globe. The emergence of information technology as a mainstream business topic was happening as I immersed myself in the stories of automation, desktop computing, software, networks, and a shifting computer landscape that was changing the world. I found myself covering the same people and companies as the *Wall Street Journal, Businessweek, Fortune,* and the *New York Times.* Indeed, we were out ahead of all those publications because *Computerworld* had staked this territory nearly two decades earlier. Sure, there was a bit of an inferiority complex being a trade journalist. The conventional wisdom of the time was that trade journals were simply rags that pandered to the individual companies within that industry sector and that the line between editorial and advertising was thin.

At *Computerworld*, nothing was further from the truth. McGovern had realized early on that the integrity of the product was the foundation of any success he might have. Advertisers wanted many eyeballs, and IT readers were drawn to the notion that when they were reading *Computerworld*, they were getting the truth, warts and all, about products, companies, and individuals. For example, during the 13-year-long IBM antitrust case, *Computerworld* set up a small office in New York just to cover the trial at the city's federal courthouse. The paper held IBM's feet to the fire, much to the chagrin of its corporate leaders, right up until the Justice Department withdrew the case in 1982.

The big computer makers occasionally pushed back, threatened to pull ads, put pressure on the company's salespeople, but McGovern always stuck by his guns. If a high-tech corporate bigwig tried to sway editorial coverage of his company, McGovern wished him well and politely declined. The decision to pull the advertising was almost always reversed after the chastened company realized that being absent from *Computerworld* hurt sales. And in a business where most trade publications were handed out for free, *Computerworld* had 120,000 paid subscribers and a pass-along readership of well over a million.

McGovern also had a global vision before globalization became the watchword of the 1990s. He had the audacity to name the company International Data Corporation (before changing Corporation to Group) when he founded it in 1964 in a small gray house in Newton, Massachusetts. The only thing international about it at the time was its proximity to the Massachusetts Turnpike, which would take you to Logan Airport where you could board an overseas flight. But McGovern had a vision about the future, and he quickly made the name true by taking those flights all over the globe, starting computer publications in one country after another, creating a vast web of locally run operations, and eventually building the company into a $3.8 billion empire with nearly 300 publications and 280 million readers worldwide.

In fact, just prior to my joining IDG, McGovern had commenced publishing *Computerworld* in China, the first Western publishing venture in that still deeply Maoist country. It was crazy, risky, and outrageous, even to IDG's board members. But McGovern was driven, committed, and undaunted. Like most hugely successful entrepreneurs, he saw opportunity where others saw roadblocks. He was fascinated with other cultures and paid close attention to countries where totalitarian regimes were collapsing, and he knew there would be a pent-up demand for information. And he rarely hesitated to make a big bet. When the Soviet Union collapsed, he was the first to start publications in the Eastern bloc nations such as Hungary, Romania, Czechoslovakia, and Poland. Though some failed, most of those bets paid off big-time, especially in China, where McGovern paved a lucrative road forward and became a favored American businessman as China entered the world markets.

Like most world-changing figures, McGovern was a study in contradictions. He was paternally generous to his employees but flinty as an old New England Yankee (even though he came from Philadelphia). Despite his wealth, he insisted on flying coach, even on long-haul flights to Asia or Australia. Woe to any employee sitting in first class if McGovern boarded the same plane. He drove an old Ford sedan, rusted and dented, until one of his executives insisted that he drive his used Mercedes, believing it was unseemly for IDG's chairman to be seen in an old beater.

Affable and welcoming, he was intensely shy by nature and had to force himself to become outgoing as his new company grew. In conversation he could seem robotic and rehearsed, but those who knew him best said he could throw down a few drinks with the best of them and get crazy after the business meetings ended. At one management meeting in the Bahamas, he had a few too many, insisted on climbing a palm tree, and had to be coaxed back down.

Complex, driven, and relentless, the only thing that could slow him down was illness, which eventually took his life at age 76 in 2014. What he built was an iconic company that thrived and grew and defied the odds for more than half a century, a company built in his image, with his values and his imprint on every corner of the organization.

I can't remember what he said to me during our brief encounter that first Christmas in the *Computerworld* offices back in 1983. My boss at the time, like all managers, had given him whispered details about some article or project I had completed so he could congratulate me on a job well done. It didn't matter that he had a verbal crib sheet with which to engage me and everyone else. What I do remember was that he looked me in the eye, listened to what I had to say, and gave me a clear message that he'd remember me from then on, no help required.

Over the next seven years, until I left the company, I had many encounters with Pat. I saved a folder full of his "Good News" notes with their rainbow logos and a short personal note thanking me or congratulating me for work well done. He seemed to truly enjoy that I had started a company volleyball league on the grounds outside our building. It embodied McGovern's "Let's try it" attitude, boosted morale, and cost virtually nothing. I definitely received a Good News note for that, and regularly regretted that I hadn't proposed a new publication or business venture instead.

Whenever I would see him, whether interviewing him for a magazine article or at an IDG reunion, I would suggest that we get together to write his book. His story, after all, was the stuff of business legend. He always laughed, patted me on the shoulder, and said, "It's not time yet. There's still so much more to do."

The IDG story never received the kind of attention companies like Apple, Google, or Facebook would receive. McGovern never became a Jobs-like industry superstar, but those who followed the information technology world knew what he meant to the explosion of that marketplace. His story is remarkable for the leadership lessons he demonstrated for 50 years. What follows is a sampling of those lessons, along with his story and the story of the company he built from little more than the seeds of a good idea. My hope is that this book correctly conveys the essence of the man who created an entire industry, touched the lives of thousands of employees, and changed the world.

1

CATALYST FOR THE FUTURE

Decades before the Internet-fueled explosion of youthful tech billionaires, Patrick J. McGovern Jr. built an empire and a legacy that generated far more than an annual spot on the *Forbes* list of richest people. McGovern built IDG into a worldwide technology media juggernaut that foretold and fueled the global information technology revolution. At its peak, IDG Communications had publications in nearly 100 countries, started an average of one new publication somewhere in the world every two months, and grew into a $3.8 billion behemoth with more than 13,000 employees around the globe.

It owned influential global brands such as *Computerworld*, *PCWorld*, *Macworld*, *InfoWorld*, *CIO*, *GamePro*, and *Network World*, spawned 460 websites, 200 mobile sites and apps, and nearly 300 print titles in business technology, consumer technology, digital entertainment, and video games. IDG gave the world the bestselling For Dummies book series, and IDC, the company's highly respected research arm, had more than 1,000 analysts who followed technology trends in more than 110 countries. IDG's conference and exhibition management team produced more than 700 events and conferences annually in 55 countries, and San Francisco–based IDG Ventures USA (now called Ridge Ventures),grew into a leading early-stage venture capital firm, the first of many IDG VC firms around the world. Today, those firms have a total of $3.6 billion under management.[1]

From an early age, this grandson of Irish immigrants had that rare combination of desire, self-confidence, and vision that marks those who emerge as the most influential of leaders. While most entrepreneurs wrestle with the dichotomy of risk versus reward, only the truly exceptional leaders are capable of approaching the inevitable chasm and leaping, without hesitation, into an opaque future. McGovern saw and shaped that future. He knew what he wanted to build. He had a vision and he dared to achieve it.

There is usually a seminal moment, a spark that ignites an irrepressible iconoclast, and in McGovern's life, it came early. One afternoon in 1953, McGovern, a student at Philadelphia's Northeast Catholic High School, chanced upon a magical book that would help catalyze his dream. As he often did, the 16-year-old, a voracious reader with an insatiable thirst for knowledge, came home from school, hopped on his bicycle, and pedaled the 13 miles to the Philadelphia public library on the Ben Franklin Parkway. He loved this library, a sanctuary for a restless, endlessly curious teenager who harbored big ambitions. He'd go there two or three times a week, poring over enlightening volumes for hours and immersing himself in countless eclectic subjects—from physics to fish breeding—before heading home in the dark.

As one of 4,800 students in a highly competitive high school, McGovern, from a blue-collar family, was looking for an edge, a way to enhance his academic résumé and ensure acceptance to a top university. He edited the school newspaper, performed in school plays, and joined Junior Achievement, where he got a firsthand immersion in running his own company. He had a deep-seated attraction to math and science, his best subjects, and on this particular library visit, he came across a book called *Giant Brains, or Machines That Think*, written by computer scientist Edmund C. Berkeley.[2]

2

Berkeley wasn't writing science fiction. As an early proponent of the nascent computer industry, he was a futurist who foresaw the day when computers would be powerful enough to augment and mimic the human brain. Published in 1949, it was among the first books to suggest that computers would someday be capable of amplifying the human mind, doing lightning-fast calculations and analysis, and drawing from massive databases to perform tasks in minutes or seconds that would take a human days or weeks. It was purely theoretical but plausible, and McGovern was staggered by the vision. A devotee of Benjamin Franklin, he had been captivated by the great man's prowess in so many disciplines and often wondered how such a brilliant, multidisciplinary mind operated, seemingly on a different plane than most people. The idea that computers would offer a means to enhance mankind's intellectual skills struck a chord with McGovern and set him on a path of discovery that would illuminate his entire remarkable career. That intersection of technology and the human brain would become a lifelong passion, triggered by Berkeley's transformative book.

Within days, taking money he had earned from his paper route, an inspired McGovern headed to the local hardware store, bought plywood boards, bell wire, carpet tacks, and linoleum strips, and fashioned a rudimentary relay-based computer. The computer played tic-tac-toe, and McGovern designed it so it would never lose. Given that this was two full decades before home computer kits became catnip for technology-obsessed teens, McGovern's intelligent machine raised more than a few eyebrows in his school. He noticed people quickly grew discouraged when playing against an unbeatable foe, so he added a circular counter to the back to ensure that every fortieth move would be random rather than preprogrammed, thus offering hope that the player could win.

McGovern submitted the computer to a local science fair and won. Some MIT alumni in the Philadelphia chapter happened to visit the fair and spotted the invention. Impressed, they approached him and suggested he apply to the famed Cambridge, Massachusetts, university. Since no one from his high school had ever gone to MIT, the priests urged him to forget such vaporous dreams and apply to Villanova or some other Jesuit school. Undaunted and willing to take the risk, a trait that would later exemplify his leadership philosophy, McGovern applied to MIT, was accepted, and received a full scholarship. In the fall of 1955, he headed to Cambridge.

MIT energized McGovern, as it did generations of the most brilliant technology thinkers. But in many ways, he was an atypical MIT student. Fueled by his fascination with "giant brains," he focused on the juxtaposition between neurophysiology, the study of how the brain works, and electronic circuitry in the emerging field of computing. He combined biology with electrical engineering in the hope that the two disciplines would forge a career building computers that could think.

"I quickly found out that there are a hundred billion neurons and a hundred trillion connections between them, and computers at that time were running on vacuum tubes or hybrid circuits," McGovern recalled. "I thought, there's no way you can analyze something as complex as the brain by using computer simulations, not at that time. But I did believe that computers someday would become supercomputers and do billions of calculations a second. Then we could make some real progress in understanding how the brain works."

Unlike most of his hyperfocused classmates, McGovern had an array of interests. Having edited his high school newspaper, he was attracted to the media—for the impact that the widespread flow of information had on humankind. After all, Ben Franklin had been a publisher, among his many vocations. McGovern thought a lot about how best to present content so that it resonated and triggered the synapses in people's brains. "How do we understand how to make the information as meaningful and enjoyable and understandable to people as possible?" he asked himself. "To do that, you have to understand how the brain works."

One day, while glancing at the student union bulletin board, the 19-year-old McGovern spotted a notice from a new magazine looking for a technical editor. The publication, *Computers and*

Automation, was the first mainstream magazine focused on computers. McGovern was intrigued. When he applied for the job, he discovered that the magazine was the brainchild of none other than Edmund Berkeley, the author who had written the book that had so inspired McGovern's interest in computing and the human brain.

Arriving in Newton, a Boston suburb, for his job interview, he told Berkeley how much he had been motivated by *Giant Brains, or Machines That Think*. Berkeley asked him some questions about the book, and then exclaimed, "You really read it! You understand it all! You're hired." A chance to work with this early computer enthusiast and futurist was thrilling for McGovern. Berkeley wasn't just a fantasist about what might happen. He was a pragmatist, among the early corporate computer users, who had worked as an actuary at a big New York insurance company using a Univac 1. He eventually founded the renowned Association for Computing Machinery (ACM), an organization for computer professionals.[3] For McGovern, it was an introduction to the nascent information technology universe.

Up to then, he had assumed he would focus on a career in biology or neuroscience research. But what became an eight-year stint at Berkeley's magazine was transformational. Early on, he was in awe of the fact that as the assistant editor of a real magazine, he could pick up the phone and call anyone in the computer industry and they would talk to him. He was, after all, still a college student. When Thomas Watson Sr. visited the MIT campus, McGovern, with his press credentials, was able to land a few minutes to interview the legendary founder of IBM.

McGovern later recalled two things Watson told him that left an indelible impression. Watson spoke about valuing employees, giving generous benefits and salaries to people, a concept that IBM introduced to corporate America. When McGovern mentioned that he'd recently returned from a trip to Iceland, Watson smiled and began to talk about IBM's manager in Reykjavík. He not only knew the fellow's name, he knew his wife's name and that he had three children. "Here's a guy running a company with 300,000 people around the world, and he knows the name of a manager in Iceland and his wife and children," McGovern said. "He really does put people first." It was a revelation and a leadership lesson McGovern would remember.

McGovern, editor of the MIT student newspaper, photographs James Killian, MIT president, who in 1957 was named President Eisenhower's science advisor at the dawn of the Sputnik era.

During his first summer at the magazine, Berkeley handed McGovern a Greyhound bus ticket. He said, "I bought you a $99 ticket for which you get unlimited travel to anywhere for 99 days. I want you to go around the country and meet the heads of the computer companies and their engineers and find out what they're planning to do. I also want you to talk to some leading computer users."

After spending his summer meeting industry luminaries and passionate technologists and having free rein to pick their brains,

McGovern had an epiphany. Instead of becoming an engineer or scientist, he would become a communicator, spreading the word like Johnny Appleseed about the coming information technology era.

When he graduated from MIT in the spring of 1959, McGovern became the full-time associate publisher of Berkeley's magazine for a whopping $60 a month, not much even in those days. The money didn't matter. He was enthralled with the editorial process. He worked for *Computers and Automation* for most of the next eight years as his interest in media and information technology grew exponentially. The influence that came with providing intellectual leadership to this suddenly burgeoning community was deeply satisfying and impossible to ignore.

INTERNATIONAL DATA

It was a cold February day trip to New York City in 1964 that brought everything into sharp focus. McGovern took the train to Manhattan for an RCA product introduction in the morning and an interview with Univac CEO Lou Rader in the afternoon.

RCA had introduced a new magnetic card memory system, and McGovern was underwhelmed. Another company had introduced something similar six months earlier, and its sales were pitiful. Why is RCA going down the same road, he wondered? When he questioned the RCA engineers about the intended application for the product, they responded, "Oh, we haven't thought about an application. We thought this would be the most clever random access memory method available." *In other words, throw a product into the marketplace and hope demand emerges.* Even in the earliest days of the computer industry, this illogical strategy was a head-scratcher for McGovern.

When he met Rader, he posed a question: Why are so many companies doing all this R&D and making products that don't have an identifiable need in the market?

"You're exactly right," Rader replied. "That's just what I worry about, that all this money is being spent without guidance from the marketplace. We don't know where the customers are or what they are doing. Right now, we try to find this out through our own sales force, but it is of limited help." Rader looked up and added, "If somebody could put together a database that described where computers were now installed, what their configurations were, what people wanted to have in the future, what are their key applications, what new peripheral devices they wanted . . . that would be very helpful."

McGovern was intrigued. At the magazine, he had compiled a count of installed computers by model and knew there were about 10,000 machines in the corporate and research worlds. He thought this broader level of information could be a valuable supplement to the magazine. He said to Rader, "I could send out questionnaires to all the organizations that have the size and scope to be a computer user and compile a database of installations, configurations, and outstanding orders." Rader replied, "Fantastic! That's just what we need. How much would you charge?"

This was 1964, and there were no benchmarks for McGovern to rely on. "About $15,000," he blurted out, pulling a number out of the ether. Rader shot back, "No. That's unacceptable!"

Thinking quickly, McGovern responded, "Well, my office is near a high school. I could probably get the high school students to do the work, to keypunch the data, and maybe I can do it for $12,000."

Rader leaned across his desk. "No, no, Pat. You don't understand. No one would trust information that is as cheap as you are proposing to provide! They wouldn't believe it had any quality or reliability. You'd have to charge a lot more, twice that, and then they'll think it's quality and they'll use it. Charge $30,000 and you'll be professional."

McGovern was stunned. "The higher the price, the more the usefulness?" he asked. "Absolutely!" Rader replied.

McGovern smiled. Rader added, "Don't only sell it to me, but offer it to the other computer companies, and you'll have many more resources to build the best database to help our industry understand the future needs in the market."

In a euphoric daze, McGovern headed to Penn Station for the train back to Boston. "The higher the price, the more the demand," he thought to himself. "I certainly like that business model." Before boarding, he placed a call to Ed Berkeley back at the magazine. McGovern explained the concept and suggested, "We'll have to make an investment to get this going." But Berkeley immediately nixed the idea. "I'm not interested in research, but if you want to do it on the side, that's fine. You just do it and take the risk yourself."

Most young journalists would have dismissed the notion of taking on such an enterprise alone. But McGovern couldn't wait to try out the concept and make it real. On the train, he wrote a project proposal and a possible questionnaire to send out. And he decided this new enterprise needed a name. Ever the pragmatist, he took out some index cards, wrote down the elements of a possible name using words like "data," "national," "computer," "systems," and more. He then shuffled the cards and picked three. Up came "international," "data," and "corporation." In that moment, International Data Corporation, or IDC, was born. Geographically, "international" extended no further than Newton, Massachusetts, but McGovern was unabashed.

"I thought that sounded like a sufficiently general name that would give me lots of freedom to move in any direction in the market," he recalled. After calling a friend at Harvard Law School, who checked and found that the appellation was unused, McGovern added the name to the proposal and typed it up over the weekend. On Monday, he mailed the document to 20 companies thinking, "I'll never hear anything about it." Instead, the mailman brought a welcome surprise. Within two weeks, he was "astonished and amazed" to receive checks from eight companies for a total of $80,000 in prepayments representing a third of the total he would garner. For someone making $60 a month, such a sum was "inconceivable."

Like any young entrepreneur faced with an influx of cash, McGovern rushed to his bank to deposit the checks in his account, but the teller stopped him. "This is a company name," she said. "You need authorization by your board of directors to open an account with us."

Suddenly, what he had thought of as a flyer had turned serious. His law school friend helped him with the process of incorporating his new venture. He asked a few friends to invest and join his board, but only his sister, Laurette, and his research assistant and future wife, Susan Sykes (whom he married in September 1964), had enough confidence to do so. They both invested $10 for 10 shares, and became, along with McGovern, the original board. He registered the company, deposited the checks, and decided he needed some base capital to get things moving, so he sold his car for $5,000. Looking back, he was immensely proud of the fact that the $10 investments from his wife and sister were eventually worth millions. And because the nascent venture began to generate cash so quickly, he never had to touch the original $5,000 base capital. "That $5,000 is still sitting there, with some interest," he boasted decades later. "I never added another dollar of base capital to it."

It would be satisfying for business folklore to claim that McGovern knew he had a tiger by the tail and quit his day job. But he stayed on as an editor at *Computers and Automation* for three more years, mixing his editorial duties with the burgeoning demands of his start-up venture. Eventually Ed Berkeley became annoyed at his young protégé's divided loyalties, and in 1967, McGovern realized that IDC required his full-time attention.

McGovern had already learned a valuable business lesson: *If you listen to what people want and respond accordingly, you will do very well.* If you focus only on what you'd *like* to do and try to force it into the marketplace, the risk of failure is high. In 1967, the computer industry was roiling with portent. Corporate customers were not only embracing computers in fast-growing numbers, but an entire new industry sector, built upon smaller, cheaper, powerful systems called minicomputers, was putting technology into the hands of end users. As products proliferated in all directions and the future of computing began to crystallize for a growing number of bright, talented entrepreneurs in Silicon Valley and Boston, the thirst for industry insight and data was insatiable. It was a demand Pat McGovern was well positioned to meet.

A NEWSPAPER FOR AN INDUSTRY

McGovern's departure from *Computers and Automation* was little more than a footnote to his epiphany of 1967. That year, as he embarked full-time on his solo venture, he started his first, and perhaps most important publication, *Computerworld*. Since he started IDC in 1964, he had been publishing a newsletter called *The EDP Industry and Market Report*, known as The Gray Sheet. For $49 a year, subscribers received detailed semimonthly reports on what the major computers makers like IBM, Burroughs, Univac, and Honeywell were selling. But McGovern foresaw a much bigger publishing opportunity.

A flourishing industry that embraced the research from IDC now required more. Most data center managers, faced with multimillion-dollar technology purchasing requirements, remained dependent on advertising literature from the computer makers— and they didn't appreciate the obvious marketing effort that offered little news, credible product data, or industry insight. What they weren't getting was any knowledge about what their colleagues in competing companies and industries were experiencing. Were their challenges and pain points similar? Did others have the same issues with product reliability? How were they training their people? There was no reliable source for answers to these questions.

In fact, there existed just one publication, a monthly magazine called *Datamation*, started in 1957 when corporate computing was in its infancy. McGovern envisioned something far more dynamic and immediate. *Computerworld* would be a weekly newspaper designed to cover the fast-changing industry with a staff of editors and reporters who would blanket the marketplace and write high-quality stories about both vendors and end users. Like any credible newspaper, *Computerworld* would report the bad news along with the good, and early headlines such as "Disk Drive Crashes, 1,000 Records Destroyed at Bank" or "Hospital Data System Loses All Its Data" shook up an industry unused to such candor and timely information.

Unlike *Datamation* and other ad-driven magazines starting to emerge within the industry, *Computerworld* would sell paid subscriptions along with advertising. In an environment where trade publications were all built upon "controlled circulation" or unpaid subscribers, McGovern decided to use Lou Rader's formula: if you make a product appear valuable, it will have instant credibility and people will pay for it. By charging a subscription fee, not only would *Computerworld* become profitable quickly, it would have the cachet and credibility that rapidly made it the bible of the information technology industry. *Computerworld*, all 12 pages of it, debuted in June 1967, at a computer expo in Boston. Within two weeks, McGovern had 20,000 paid subscribers on board. In short order, the publication began to grow beyond his wildest dreams. His passion for communicating information that could change people's lives had found its essential building block.

Computerworld marked the beginning of a frenzied period of growth and expansion that spawned a long list of leadership challenges that McGovern would stare down throughout the next five decades. In an industry bursting with brilliant young minds and a tsunami of new ideas that would change the world, high-quality leadership, that rare but indispensable ingredient, would mark the key difference between the winners and losers.

BUILDING THE EMPIRE

Embracing globalization before the term was popularized, McGovern boarded a plane to Japan in 1971 to start his first overseas publication, and to his colleagues, it seemed like he never disembarked. McGovern renamed the company International Data

CATALYST FOR THE FUTURE

COMPUTERWORLD

The Newsweekly for the Computer Community

Vol. 1, No. 1   Cambridge, Massachusetts,   June 21, 1967   25 Cents

COMPUTERWORLD IS LAUNCHED

First Newspaper For The Full Computer Community

Burroughs 3500 Software Shown Publicly

BOSTON, June 20th — Burroughs Corporation showed a 70K 3500 computer here today doing a complicated series of multi-programming operations under the Advanced Operating System. At times five user programs were being simultaneously executed, and a major point of the demonstration was to show the low overhead involved when one program was introduced over already operating programs. Programs demonstrated included COBOL compilations, and remote inquiries as well as standard batch processing and tape sorting operations.

This demonstration marked the first public showing of the 3500 hardware and software, although private press showings have been given earlier this year. There was a greater interest than usual in the demonstration because the software for the 3500 — including the operating system itself — was basically running on a B 3500 before the 3500 hardware was ready. Burroughs claims that the first program ran under the operating system the same day that the hardware was delivered — and that multi-programming started within the month.

Core Advantages

Spectators following the demonstrations this afternoon through the colored flip-chart appeared visibly impressed both by the fact that Burroughs was demonstrating such an advanced system 14 months after the original announcements of the 2500, 3500 systems — and by the apparent efficiency of the system. The arrangement of core memory modules was also commented on favorably, one manager saying that it was a lot more practical than on his present system. "With this system" he said, "even if I do blow my core, it only involves another 10K bytes. With my present system such a move would involve dumping my core."

COMPUTERS TO SOLVE CONGO'S PROBLEMS ?

The importation of an American computer is being arranged by General Joseph Mobutu, Congolese President, to solve many of the problems of the African trouble spot. Instancing double billing, the President said that using the computer in control and check on fund availability would prevent various financial abuses by provincial governments, and other quasi-independent agencies

COBOL, RPG Bested By New Language ?

A new computer language, which competes with COBOL and RPG and is presently operational on IBM 1401 and System 360/30s and up, has been described by Statistical Tabulating Company Inc. which is marketing it through its nation-wide chain of service centers. Developed by Applied Data Systems of San Francisco, the new language is called ADPAC and has been used for the past six months by STAT/TAB for all its own in-house work.

During this period it is said to have cut programming and compilation time drastically, while leaving object-time essentially unaffected.

The new language appears to gain its efficiency differently when compared to COBOL than when RPG are considered. In the case of COBOL the great advantage comes in the elimination of the Data Division. This particular feature of COBOL, which has practically survived intact from the early days of automatic programming over a decade ago, has always been a stumbling block for efficient programming of small programs.

In the past there have been a number of attempts to eliminate it, but it is still one of the four untidy divisions of the COBOL standard programs, and shows no signs of being phased out. WIG regard to RPG the efficiency of the ADPAC language is gained by providing additional language elements, in particular a 'Do' loop function, equivalent to the COBOL 'Perform' verb.

Frank J. Burns, Stat-Tabs National Director of Research & Development talking to your COMPUTERWORLD reporter this week explained the lack of change in object-time performance noted within his own operation was due to the fact that they were normally input-output bound no matter how they were programmed. Documentation provided by Mr. Burns stated that ADPAC's programs are at last as fast and up to 35% faster in execution speed.

While ADPAC is presently operational only on IBM computers, it is said to be hardware independent and to be suitable for Honeywell Series 200, RCA Spectra 70 and Univec 9300 systems. Previous announcements of ADPAC's availability on the Honeywell Series 200 have now been withdrawn, and no firm date for the Series 200 ADPAC was immediately available. However, it appears likely that it will be ready this fall.

The price of ADPAC to a user is normally $15,000 for the first year at the primary site, with a support type charge of $1,000 per year thereafter. Secondary sites within the same organization can be supplied at a lesser rate. The system is being marketed both by Applied Data Systems and by Statistical Tabulating Corp.

Details of the comparative performance of ADPAC on IBM 1401 and 360/30 computers are included in the 'IBM Items' on Page 8, together with other information of primary interest to IBM users.

Next Issue Next Month Weekly In September

READERSHIP TARGET 300,000

BOSTON, June 20th — Considerable interest was raised today with the announcement of a weekly newspaper for the computer community. The announcement was made as the DPMA exhibition opened this afternoon, and conversation buzzed around the small COMPUTERWORLD exhibit — and other places in the hall — as to its prospects. Visitors to the exhibit were able to examine a prototype issue which had been produced to alert the advertising area to the new publication. Almost without exception the basic idea of such a newsweekly was accepted although there were some disparaging remarks made about the typography and style of the prototype. Everyone was agreed, however, that they were looking forward to seeing the first issue, which was due to the COMPUTERWORLD stand the next day.

Patrick J. McGovern, publisher of the newsweekly, explained that the aim of this publication was to bring news while it is news' to the people involved in computer-related work. Waving a copy of the June issue of a well-known computer magazine, he pointed to the 'News' section which had items which were between six weeks and two months old and noted that the magazine had only been delivered. For example, this IBM 1130 announcement", he said, 'was released by IBM on April 17th, the day before the SJCC — over two months ago. It's unreasonable for people in a fast moving area like the computer field to have their current awareness limited by such 'horse-and-buggy' delays. The computer field is entering its third decade, yet its communications media are not providing the timely information service needed by people working as professionals in data processing. It is this need which COMPUTERWORLD is designed to fulfill'.

McGovern explained that quick turn-around time was the critical element in the planning of COMPUTERWORLD. 'Everything was made secondary to that' he said. 'I don't expect that we have covered every possibility — but we have done quite a lot of things expressly to speed the news to the people.' Pressed for instances, he cited the printing time — Thursday evenings. That way we can get the addressed copies into the mail on Tuesday morning — about 3 a.m. This coincides with an activity low point in the post office's operations, and helps them service COMPUTERWORLD. Other points he cited include the weekly service, and the paid distribution. Both of these are necessary, he said, in order to get the best post office treatment which he said was needed.

Editor Alan Taylor did not quite agree that turn-around-time was the top priority. 'It's a top-priority item, true,' he commented, 'but technical honesty, and readability are equally important. We'll keep our deadlines — but it will be at the cost of lost sleep rather than any quality letdown.'

Criticism of Prototype

Taylor said that he had heard some criticism of the prototype issue. Using a copy pushed on the exhibit to illustrate his points he said that the style of the paper had been attacked. It had been compared to a house organ — or to 'something the government might put out'. The use of many different typefaces has also been said to be 'disturbing'. 'I don't really know yet what the readers want, ' he said. 'I do know that typography is important, and that we are trying our best to use it to help the paper's readability. We think that using different faces will keep the different stories separated from each other — but if the readers don't like it we will change. We're not proud!'

Ann Babel, COMPUTERWORLD's production manager, when contacted at the lay-out boards where she was preparing for the Tuesday night printing of the first issue of COMPUTERWORLD, gave a different slant on the matter. 'Well — it WAS a house organ' she said. 'It was designed to introduce COMPUTERWORLD — and that's about as house organy as anything I can think of. There certainly were some faces we should not have used; but that first issue was prepared on the same time-schedule as we hope to keep in the future. It was a necessary experiment to prove our capabilities to ourselves — and I think it was 80% successful. Now we are working hard on the other 20%.'

Visitors to the Stand

Visitor's opinions seemed more concerned with the content of the paper than with the mechanics. One DP manager — pointing to an article on a new proprietary language — said 'That's the sort of stuff I want — because it may well solve my problems — and I can't see my salesman telling me about it. He'd have to try to explain why his firm hadn't

(Continued on Page 6)

DPMA, 1967

The Computer Community owes a debt of gratitude to the DP for its pioneering work with the Certificate of Data Processing — surely one of the most significant items of computerdom's second decade — and for its annual shows. These shows, and the seminars and workshops connected with them are particularly suitable to practical day-to-day problems which users find so important.

The 1967 DPMA Show is now with us, and COMPUTERWORLD presents a special photographic two page spread on Pages 4 and 5 of this issue as its tribute to a very worthwhile organization — the Data Processing Management Association.

Debut issue of *Computerworld*, 1967.

13

Group, or IDG, to create a broader, truly global canvas on which to paint his masterpiece. He designated the name IDC for the company's original research arm.

Those who joined this unique firm as young, eager participants in the embryonic technology upsurge got more than a job. McGovern created a culture rather than a workplace, and as venture capitalist Fred Wilson said, "Culture is destiny. You can get everything else right, but if you get your culture wrong, you are going to have problems."

McGovern got IDG's culture right. He cultivated, developed, and protected it for half a century. Few founders can claim such successful longevity. IDG alumni, those who got their start in technology journalism or marketing, make up a virtual Who's Who of industry influencers. While most early entrepreneurs in the tech revolution shone brightly and then faded quickly, McGovern managed to stay ahead of countless technology trends by hiring smart, young, and aggressive talent, providing enthusiastic support, and stepping out of the way.

George Colony, founder and chairman of Forrester Research, a leading technology research firm, has been an outspoken witness of the technology revolution. He deeply admired McGovern for his vital role in shaping that revolution.

"If you look at the history of the technology industry over the last 40 years, he was a fundamental part of that story in that he created the publishing industry that supported, advertised, analyzed, and publicized the growth of that industry," Colony said. "We really wouldn't have been able to understand the architecture of the Apple II or IBM's corporate networks within large corporations without Pat McGovern because IDG was educating the world about all those products and companies. Every industry needs that megaphone and he was the tech industry's megaphone for all these years."[4]

What set McGovern apart from so many successful moguls who dominated various industry sectors was the breadth of his skills and his persistence, over 50 years, in relentlessly pursuing his goals. He wasn't only interested in educating and informing people about machines that think, which resulted in IDG. He was also deeply fascinated by the *original* human brain and how it worked, which, in 2000, led him and his second wife, Lore Harp McGovern, to give a $350 million gift to MIT, one of the largest gifts in the history of academic philanthropy, for the creation of the McGovern Institute for Brain Research (MIBR). McGovern wanted to establish an environment in which the latest technology could come together with world-class brain researchers to fuel a deeper understanding of brain disorders and find cures for serious neurological diseases. He approached the MIBR with the same unique, hands-on leadership qualities that he brought to IDG.

HOW DID HE DO ALL THIS?

The road to the future, now as when McGovern began his enterprise, is littered with good intentions and missed opportunities. But this merely serves to illuminate how remarkable Pat McGovern's story truly is. Getting it so right for so long is the stuff of a rare and notable journey. Along the way, he emphatically offered up a collection of leadership lessons worthy of serious attention.

The chapters that follow offer an exploration of 10 of those vital leadership lessons. As you will see, the essential significance of each applies to any organization in a wide range of industries. Great leadership and insight transcends corporate boundaries, and applied with wisdom, these lessons offer a potent starting place for any existing or start-up enterprise to drive the future forward.

LESSON ONE
Have a Mission That Matters, and Let People Know You Are on That Mission Together

*If you listen to what people want and
you respond, then you do very well.*
—PAT MCGOVERN

Of all the leadership lessons he took to heart during his long career, McGovern intuitively grasped one of the most important early in his career. In order to build a successful enterprise, you have to identify a clear mission from the outset and find effective ways to share that mission with your people. Before Google and Facebook turned hiring into a science and carefully screened every new hire, McGovern pulled together an eclectic and enthusiastic group of young employees for his fledgling company in a less analytical but highly effective manner. He shared the goals and strategies, but he imparted the *mission*—to propagate the benefits, understanding, and acceptance of information technology around the world—through sheer determination and passion for what he was doing. New employees got swept up by this large man with an outsized dream.

For example, when he was 23 years old, Burgess Needle lived in the gray house at 355 Walnut St. in Newtonville, Massachusetts. A student at a junior college across the street, Needle rented an upstairs room from McGovern, who owned the house and had reserved the first floor for his start-up, International Data Corp. It was 1964, and McGovern was just a few years older than Needle but had the ambition of a seasoned business veteran.

On that first floor, McGovern had created his first industry report, which was essentially a census of all the mainframe computers installed in the United States. With IDC up and running, McGovern accelerated his already ambitious efforts. IDC would become celebrated for its role in counting all the world's computers, a staple of its practice to this day. But for McGovern, this was just a beginning. He foresaw a burgeoning audience for market share data and forecasts. In order to create a steady revenue stream, he created The Gray Sheet, which found a big audience among computer makers and their corporate customers who were seeking vital information about the nascent technology landscape.

The Gray Sheet was the first publication of what would become a global publishing empire, but its humble beginnings offered a glimpse of McGovern's tenacity in creating the mission that would drive him for the next 50 years. He wrote the newsletter himself from data gathered by a tiny staff of young part-time stringers, and his new assistant, Susan Sykes (who would soon become his wife), typed up his notes. The youthful staffers were on the phone calling the giant computer vendors and their customers to gather as much information as they could about computer installations.

In the first issue, dated March 23, 1964, McGovern laid out an impressively detailed look at the computer industry landscape, a marketplace dominated by IBM but with an array of hungry and aggressive competitors. "From all indications," McGovern wrote,

"1964 will certainly be a turning point year in the development of the American computer industry." Indeed, as more and more corporate, government, military, and academic institutions began installing these massive computers, the information technology industry was in the midst of explosive growth. McGovern knew he was tapping into something potent and lucrative—a game-changing shift in both business and society.

The lead story trumpeted a yet-unnamed new IBM computer system, predicted to debut in April. The headline noted that IBM "Expects to Install 5000 of Its New Computer Systems in Next Five Years." McGovern, who'd been editor of both his high school and college newspapers, boldly predicted sales of more than $3.5 billion for Big Blue over that period, a stunning figure for any manufacturer in those days. The new computer turned out to be the IBM System/360, the first "family" of small to large computers, which would transform the industry.

That first issue also promised a monthly assessment of sales from all of the computer makers, including major competitors such as Honeywell, Univac, Control Data, Burroughs, and RCA, along with critical analysis of each company's sales efforts. Given the dearth of such vital information, he found a ready audience more than willing to pay.

"What struck me was his work ethic," Needle, now a Vermont-based poet and librarian, recalled about McGovern. "He would be there day after day, morning till night, 16 to 18 hours, putting together the newsletter. I'd be upstairs, but one time I walked downstairs at three in the morning and there was Pat ready to go out for a run. He was wearing a T-shirt, running shorts, and running shoes. He said, 'I'm too revved up. I have to work this off,' and he went up to the track at the local high school and ran a few laps to clear his head. He came back, showered, and went right back to work. His energy was unreal."

Needle, a liberal arts major and budding writer, had worked at a local deli, but one day the deli burned down, and he was out of a job. McGovern said, "Come work for me." Needle responded,

"I don't know what I can do for you." Computers and math were anathema to him. But McGovern suggested he take a generic aptitude test to see if he was qualified. Reluctantly, Needle agreed. The test got progressively more difficult as it went along, treading into logic, semantics, and other esoteric fields.

"There were 33 questions," Needle said. "By the time I reached 28, I just stopped and said, 'This is as far as I can go.' Pat glanced at it and said, 'You're hired.'"

McGovern explained that anyone who scored over 27 would be bored out of their mind by the work. Under 17 and they wouldn't be up for it. "You had 23 correct," he said to Needle, "so you are perfect."

Needle joined the young company as a part-time employee. He cold-called companies up and down the Eastern Seaboard and, using a questionnaire McGovern had written, asked the data processing managers what kind of equipment they had, what they were doing with the equipment, and what their needs were. Needle wondered why these giant computer vendors would buy data from this tiny unknown start-up operating in a tranquil Boston suburb. Didn't they have their own resources to get the information? And why would data processing executives talk to him about proprietary corporate information such as their inventory of computer equipment? McGovern told him, "They'll talk because they are proud. They'll be delighted to share this information. These are people who don't have the opportunity to share with anybody. You'll have to shut them up." And he was correct.

McGovern, reacting to his recent conversation with the CEO of Univac, only saw opportunity. "We need this information," the Univac chief had told him, and McGovern saw quickly that he was right. His research might seem like small change to these giants, but it could spawn bountiful leads for their sales forces. It was audacious, and it worked.

His readers, who were eventually willing to pay upward of $500 a year for a subscription, were on board because the information was scarce, timely, and valuable.

"I would see him on the phone with people trying to track down a rumor about a new high-speed printer or some other computer peripheral, and you could tell the person was not very forthcoming," Needle said. "Pat would talk, tell a joke, circle back, and finally he'd smile, tap the desk, and I would think, 'Got it.'"

A POTENT OPPORTUNITY

At age 27, McGovern displayed the kind of doggedness and risk-taking spirit that would characterize a later generation of Silicon Valley entrepreneurs. From the first days, he understood his mission, and the company coalesced around that mission. Burgess Needle stayed with the start-up for less than a year, choosing instead to pursue a literary career. But tens of thousands of others, from California to Beijing, would eventually join IDG and embrace McGovern's mission. The people he hired learned fast, bought in, and became expert in their various industry niches. He had an almost mythical persona that attracted these young, talented writers, editors, artists, and salespeople who propelled the company to the top of the flourishing information technology media industry.

Just three years after he founded the company, in June 1967, McGovern published the first issue of *Computerworld*, a weekly newspaper that chronicled the news and events shaping the now mushrooming computer industry. In so doing, he took IDC into the emerging technology publishing arena, established a brand that would quickly become a dominant force in the industry, and began a period of sustained and phenomenal growth.

A scientist by nature, McGovern believed in the data. He was among the first in the computer industry to understand the value of surveying professionals in the information technology field. *Computerworld* emerged, not on a whim, but from listening to these early computer users voice their concerns. McGovern recalled an early research project IDC was conducting for a client to identify the sources of information for people who bought computer systems.

"We went down and interviewed about 40 people who were data center heads or computer center heads," he said. "They were all telling us the same story. They said, 'I get a tremendous amount of literature from the manufacturers.'" These computer makers and their marketing and advertising campaigns, replete with the biases of companies pushing their own products and agendas, seemed to be the sole source of information for prospective buyers.

"What I don't get,'" said one data processing manager, "is visibility as to what my colleagues are doing. Because I know that they're having the same concerns about acquiring and using this equipment effectively and well, and problems with some of the reliability of the equipment, and how to train their people. It is a shared challenge for us."

The trigger for McGovern came next. "There isn't anyone who keeps us connected as a community, who keeps us up to date and aware," the manager added. "There are so many things happening, we'd really like to get high frequency information."

Hearing that, McGovern saw through the frustration and angst to a potent opportunity. A weekly newspaper, staffed with talented journalists and editors, could find a ready audience, an audience willing to pay a subscription fee to get the timely and discerning information they needed. In creating *Computerworld*, McGovern set a new template for his mission.

He changed the company's name to International Data Group, split IDC into a separate research arm, and soon after decided to legitimize the "International" in the company name by taking his vision overseas. The mission crystallized. IDG would provide information services *about information technology*, and though the elasticity of the objective allowed for occasional twists and turns, the ultimate success was built upon a steadfast devotion, over the next half-century, to the core mission. It was a lesson from which McGovern would rarely deviate.

A TECHNOLOGY BEACHHEAD

As CEO of Herman Miller, Max De Pree, an innovative business leader, authored *Leadership Is an Art*, a management book that sold more than 800,000 copies. As De Pree wrote, "The first responsibility of a leader is to define reality. The last is to say thank you. In between, the leader is a servant and a debtor." Few were as good at defining reality for their mission as Pat McGovern.

As he traveled hundreds of thousands of air miles each year for much of his adult life, McGovern was a focused and passionate evangelist for his vision of a world connected by technology. Well before it became fashionable, he saw the benefits of the information technology revolution and realized that, as it was changing the world, it would soon become the biggest industry in the world—bigger than automobiles, bigger than oil and gas, bigger than banking.

Today, in a market where tech companies such as Apple, Amazon, Google, and Facebook are among the most valuable entities in the Fortune 500, this perception hardly raises eyebrows. But when McGovern foresaw this, in the late 1960s and early 1970s, it was hardly a fait accompli. Few envisioned the exponential growth of technology on such an enormous scale. For McGovern, there was no doubt.

Pat Kenealy, a venture capitalist and former CEO of IDG, remembers seeing McGovern speak to a publishing industry group in 1978. "The IT business is this big, and it is growing this fast," Kenealy recalled McGovern telling the audience. "It spends between 1 percent and 2 percent of its revenues on marketing and communication. Therefore, this is a huge and fast-growing advertising business for us. People will need to subscribe to this kind of information because the revolution is so big and so fast-growing, and advertisers will need to explain to prospective buyers what they are doing."

The business was growing so fast, in fact, that a good media company "must make a lot of money to keep up with the mission." IDG had to be profitable to grow and to serve the industry. Though some have come to wonder whether this technological revolution has been as positive as advertised—automation stealing jobs, video games stealing childhoods, foreign governments stealing e-mails—McGovern never wavered in his belief that it was good for the planet and good for the individual.

With his enthusiasm and unflagging belief in his mission, McGovern managed to jump-start an entire industry aimed at understanding the emerging technology revolution of the second half of the twentieth and beginning of the twenty-first centuries. With IDG ascending to the height of its influence, a 1988 front-page profile in the *Christian Science Monitor* declared, "Rupert Murdoch reigns over racy tabloids. Dow Jones keeps the diary of the American dream. But Patrick McGovern probably has more influence over computers than anyone else in the world."[1] A year later, a *New York Times* profile called McGovern "the prophet for his age."[2]

So effective was his message that he brought thousands of employees, hundreds of thousands of customers, and millions of readers along with him. Keeping in mind that he set off on his mission in the 1960s, in the early days of the computer revolution, McGovern's ability to spread this gospel and stay the course for nearly five decades was remarkable. Kenealy pointed out that all big American industrial and social revolutions have a media company inextricably intertwined with the movement. Crane Publishing in the automobile business: Penton in oil and gas, McGraw-Hill in aerospace, Walter Annenberg in television, and of course, IDG in information technology.

The entrepreneurs who tend to emerge as legends share one key characteristic: a deep, abiding obsession with their stated mission. Beyond the inevitable riches that these successful ventures generate, what drives them is the insatiable desire to change the world, to create something indelible, and to ride the adrenaline rush that comes with building the organization to do that.

Pat McGovern simply loved what he did. In many ways, his company was his family and his life. He was laser-focused on information technology, and he became the Homer of the technology era, chronicling a remarkable odyssey from the glass-enclosed data centers housing giant mainframes to the advent of the Internet, wireless, broadband, and a world in which individuals around the globe cradle pocket-sized supercomputers in their hands.

The lesson he taught his legion of acolytes was based on a simple but valuable premise: In a fast-changing business, *long-term vision plus short-term operational excellence will outperform any other strategy.* He never believed in three-to-five-year strategic plans. He never hitched IDG's fortunes to a single technology trend, preferring to acknowledge that each new era was just another wave to surf toward the shore.

"When people compare *Computerworld* from 1970, 1980, and 1990, they say, 'The subject matter is completely different.' We say, 'Yes, but the audience is the same. We are serving the same person. It's just that their information needs evolve as the technology and applications evolve,'" McGovern said.

Mainframes gave way to minicomputers, which gave way to personal computers, which inevitably ushered in the era of portable computing and smart devices such as the iPhone and iPad. Companies came and went, some lasting a century or more, others disappearing like comets scorching across the horizon. Superstars rose at regular intervals, from Thomas Watson to Ken Olsen to Bill Gates to Steve Jobs to Jeff Bezos and Mark Zuckerberg. McGovern's career outlasted nearly all of them.

It is one thing for the founder to be zealous about his mission. It is something else entirely to build an organization filled with people who are willing to adopt that mission as their own. When Steve Jobs tried to convince John Sculley to leave a high-level job at Pepsi-Cola in 1983 to come and run Apple, he famously said, "Do you want to sell sugar water for the rest of your life, or do you want to come with me and change the world?"

McGovern's approach was more subtle. From the earliest days, through charisma, persuasion, and sheer passion for his young company, he was able to attract a growing army of employees who wholeheartedly bought into the mission.

"The fact that you have dedicated, passionate people who feel that everyone in their company is only interested in one objective works much better, and their revenue and profits go way up," he said. He eschewed the conventional wisdom of business leaders that he ought to incessantly enlarge his company, preferring instead to allow a raft of smaller, effective business units to make up the organization. Once a business got to 200 people, he divided it up into two or three groups. He was convinced that the mission was better served by people working in a group where they knew their value, knew everybody on the team, and knew exactly what they were achieving and why.

Over IDG's first decade, a set of 10 corporate values evolved. For McGovern, the values became clear after 10 years "of experiencing what works and what doesn't work, what makes successful companies continue to be successful, and not have a flame-out after one good product or service." Soon enough, every IDG office around the world sported a plaque listing the values:

1. Remain dedicated to our mission of providing exceptional information services on information technology.
2. Show respect for the dignity of each individual.
3. Invest in our people through training and career development.
4. Produce products of the highest quality.
5. Strive for excellence in customer service.
6. Keep close to our customers and qualified prospects.
7. Be responsive to changes in our marketplace.
8. Keep the corporate staff lean.
9. Encourage autonomy through a decentralized management style via locally managed business units.
10. Foster an action-oriented "Let's try it" attitude.

When he joined IDG in 1985, Londoner Keith Arnot, having come from a job in public accounting, found IDG's culture and corporate values "incredibly refreshing." Arnot, who eventually became IDG's international controller and has spent more than 30 years with the company, was impressed by the mission.

"You usually come across businesses that want to succeed by making profits, and for sure, that was a key part of Pat's objective," Arnot said. "But what he really wanted was to pursue a mission, which was to improve the quality of mankind by improving the decision making and making sure the information was available for people to make the right decisions. In a way, he had quite a humanitarian North Star."

LIVING THE MISSION

Before the term *empowerment* became a cliché, McGovern empowered his employees to stretch beyond their own self-made boundaries and turn ideas into real businesses. Ted Bloom was a high school student in Newton who was hired to work in the IDG mailroom in 1967. Working part-time as he completed his college degree, Bloom made his way to the finance department and was soon running the credit department.

"I always found the company to be challenging. It was challenging for all of us," Bloom recalled. "We were always doing things that nobody had ever done before. We just figured it out as we went along."

Bloom, who retired in 2017 as IDG's president and CFO after 50 years with the company, had the opportunity to witness McGovern's remarkable impact on people over time.

"It was his great style and love for the people and the sticking to his mission" that underscored his success, Bloom said about McGovern. "He never tried to do other things, to buy other businesses. His commitment was to the employees and how he felt that the employees were the assets of the company" who accomplished the mission.

As he expanded his empire around the world, McGovern believed that no region or country was out of reach. His entrance into China in 1980 was marked by a recognition that other Western companies had failed in this emerging market because they didn't understand the importance of personal relationships in Chinese business. McGovern made more than 130 trips to China, learned the culture, and most of all, treated IDG's Chinese employees with the same respect and caring that he did all of the company's employees.

"He made us feel that it was a family," said Tang Baoxing, one of the original editors and later vice president at *China Computerworld*, recalling the first visits from McGovern. "Our education taught us that capitalism exploits the workers, but he was so different from the propaganda. He was very kind because he was a good man, and so we were willing to work with him. He was our teacher. He taught us how to sell publications."

McGovern was equally adept at connecting with everyone in the organization, from those in the production department to the senior executives he was able to recruit. In France, for example, he turned around an impending disaster by enlisting a talented executive named Axel Leblois to embrace IDG's mission.

Having launched *Le Monde Informatique* in France in 1980, McGovern was upset when the publication's progress stalled and it began hemorrhaging money. Unlike some of the other European markets, France was challenging due to local cultural and business attitudes that differed greatly from the United States. McGovern sought a new leader. When he was introduced to Leblois, a suave young Frenchman working for Russell Reynolds, the global search firm, he explained that he was not interested in hiring the firm, he wanted to hire Leblois. Having successfully launched a computer publication earlier in his career, Leblois had the credentials McGovern sought: the ability to make a publication profitable.

Leblois signed on, quickly helped turn around the struggling publication, and became a McGovern disciple. McGovern soon asked him to run other European markets. In particular, he asked

Leblois to lead the effort to get IDG into markets behind the Iron Curtain, which in the mid-1980s remained a daunting task.

They started with Hungary, a country bristling with a yearning for information technology and populated by some of the brightest technical minds in Europe. McGovern believed there would be a ready market for technology publications. Leblois hired a Hungarian, found partners, and involved the government ministry of planning to launch the publication. In a joint venture with the Hungarian government, the new publication was profitable from day one. The government minister assured him that there would be no censorship. A year later, the same minister enlisted Leblois and IDG to help the country launch a stock market. Though it was off-mission, McGovern approved the effort, believing that it would further IDG's ability to spread the gospel about information technology.

McGovern's steadfast dedication to IDG's mission left an indelible mark on a cadre of IDG executives over the decades. Many would leave and assume leadership roles in other organizations, never forgetting the lessons they took from IDG. A corporate mission, as crucial as it is to success, is only as dynamic as the leader pushing it forward. McGovern's mission was fueled by a ceaseless desire to push the boundaries, go to levels others feared as unattainable, and drive into markets, such as China, that others refused to consider.

TAKEAWAYS

▶▶ A leader with aspirations for long-term success must define a clear mission early in the game.

▶▶ The mission must be the core driver of everything the company does, remaining strong and consistent over time and through periods of gains and losses.

▶▶ Hire people who are talented and passionate about the mission.

▶▶ The means to achieve the mission may be adjusted based on geography, markets, and personnel, but it shouldn't be compromised for any of these reasons. The mission should work as well in China as in Europe as in the United States.

▶▶ Live a set of corporate values built around the mission. Make sure employees embrace the values and propagate them around the globe.

LESSON TWO
Forge a Path on the Road Less Traveled

I shall be telling this with a sigh
Somewhere ages and ages hence:
Two roads diverged in the wood, and I—
I took the one less traveled by,
And that made all the difference.
—ROBERT FROST

Pat McGovern's career was an odyssey. There was no road less traveled in his life; he traveled *all* roads all the time in a quest to spread IDG's gospel worldwide. McGovern's father, who helped build US military bases around the globe during World War II, tempered his long absences by sending his son postcards from Japan, Morocco, Bermuda, Iceland, and many other exotic locales. McGovern once said that these postcards triggered an insatiable thirst for seeing the world. Throughout his career, his wanderlust never wavered.

When he traveled, McGovern saw the world through a unique set of lenses. Every stop was a potential business opportunity and a chance to further his vision of bringing vital information to people in every corner of the world. He believed he could build a big, financially successful company while fulfilling his mission. He was fascinated with foreign cultures and had a ceaseless desire to better understand human nature and the motivations that made people tick.

In 1960, just a year out of MIT, McGovern traveled throughout Europe with a high school classmate and fellow honor student named Jim Short. Short was already in England doing postgraduate work, and the pair decided to meet up, along with another American friend named Joyce Gleason, a Wellesley College undergraduate, to tour the continent. While most young Americans were content to see Paris and Rome, McGovern convinced his companions to venture into the Soviet Union during the height of Cold War tensions. Already entranced by the promise of computers and information technology to spread knowledge to all corners of the world, McGovern wanted to see for himself what a country ruled by a totalitarian regime looked like.

While traveling near Leningrad, the trio was picked up by the Soviet police for being too close to a sensitive military installation. Having talked their way out of that predicament, they headed to Moscow and made the dubious decision to hand out copies of *Amerika*, a US State Department magazine that extolled the virtues of American life, to a crowd outside the famed Hotel Metropol. They were immediately arrested. While Short demanded permission to call the American embassy, McGovern slipped away in the confusion and alerted the embassy, which sent an official to negotiate for the trio's release. McGovern, Gleason, and Short were ordered to leave the Soviet Union. They headed to Romania, but the experience stayed with McGovern.[1] The Russian leaders believed in the virtues of withholding information from their citizens, and McGovern foresaw a world where technology would make it increasingly difficult to assert such control.

He also had a penchant for seeking out potentially lucrative markets, regardless of the obstacles that might deter others. In 1978, with IDG growing at a rapid clip and *Computerworld* essentially printing money for the company, McGovern set his sights on China, a massive, impoverished nation just stirring from decades of economic and cultural stagnation under Mao Zedong and an oppressive communist regime. Always an admirer of the Chinese people he met in the United States, whom he found to be successful in math, engineering, and the sciences, McGovern believed information technology would be of great interest in China, perhaps not immediately but soon enough. "I dreamed that if I was ever going to fulfill our mission of being able to help hundreds of millions of people with information, I had better get involved in China as early as possible," he said.

On a business trip to Japan for a board meeting of Japan *Computerworld*, McGovern planned to stop in Moscow, his old stomping grounds, to attend a computer exposition. He noticed there was a flight from Tokyo to Moscow with a stopover in Beijing, and despite the obvious regulatory obstacles, he booked it. His intention was to get off the plane in Beijing, spend a day in the city, and then take the same flight the following day to Moscow.

Given that the United States and China did not yet have diplomatic relations, McGovern's plan was ambitious, if not downright foolhardy. Americans were scarce in Beijing, and those determined to visit needed to traverse daunting levels of clearance. Somewhat naively, he didn't worry about being arrested or detained. He thought he might have to stay at the airport, but the opportunity to set foot in China was too alluring to pass up. At the airport in Tokyo, the gate agent immediately asked for his visa to visit China. McGovern quickly replied in his signature upbeat manner, "Oh no. I don't need a visa. I'm only in transit."

The gate agent wasn't fooled. "There is no transit," he said. Deciding he should push the envelope, McGovern countered with, "Oh yes, my airline reservation people checked this out and there's no problem." Incredibly, he was allowed to board the plane. But prior to takeoff, the airline sent a small contingent of company representatives aboard to confront him with a sheaf of documents. They said, "Mr. McGovern, before this plane leaves, you must sign waivers of liability for this airline." If he was caught violating international travel regulations, they wanted no responsibility.

When the flight landed in Beijing, he stepped off the plane into a Quonset-like terminal and said to himself, "They can't put me back on that plane." When he handed over his passport at customs, the agent demanded "Visa? Visa?" He shot back, "Transit, transit. I am only staying one day. Tomorrow evening I leave by air flight." Unprepared for a large, determined, undocumented American, the customs agents huddled in a back room for 20 minutes of heated discussion and returned with a piece of rice paper. It was a handwritten visa. In broken English, they instructed him to clip the paper into his passport, and to tear it up when he left. "Never tell anyone where you got this," they warned. Remarkably, he was allowed to visit downtown Beijing.

MULES AND CAMELS

The Beijing McGovern encountered was a massive city just embarking on a dramatic transformation. Westerners still called the city Peking, but that would soon change. Beijing today is a smog-engulfed modern metropolis with 21.5 million people, sky-scrapers rising across miles of cityscape, and millions of cars choked in gridlock traffic. In the decade between 2000 and 2010, the population grew by 44 percent!

In 1978, by contrast, the city had just over 8 million residents, the early rumblings of a new construction boom, a few automobiles, and millions of bicycles, which served as the preferred method of transportation. Sharing the streets were donkey carts, horse-drawn wagons, and countless two-wheeled tractor carts with high handlebars. There were mules and even camels brought in by merchants from Mongolia. The absence of color was startling.

Everyone wore the same drab gray and blue Mao-era uniforms and caps, and the sight of this tall American businessman strolling down the city streets must have turned every head.

In China then, 81 percent of the population lived in rural areas, mired in deep poverty. The poverty level was $63 a year, which translated into an income of 17 cents a day for more than 250 million rural Chinese, or more than 30 percent of the population.[2] Even in the cities, food was being rationed, higher education was available only to a small percentage of the population, and the idea of China emerging as a serious player in the modern world seemed like a pipe dream. Development under new Chinese leader Deng Xiaoping started to grow rapidly. However, in a nation with nearly a billion people, electricity use was less than that of Japan or Ukraine.

"Everyone thought the Chinese had lost both the passion and the talent for doing anything to build an economy," said Rao Yi, director of the McGovern Institute for Brain Research at Peking University. "No one could have imagined China would go the way we did economically over the last 30 years. Most Chinese would have thought that Pat McGovern was wasting his time and money in China."

But 1978 was also the year of the Beijing Spring, when the Chinese government loosened its iron grip and allowed people to experience and learn about the outside world. Young people, driven to think independently by their bitter experiences during the Cultural Revolution, began to publish journals and put up wall posters, especially at "democracy wall" in the heart of Beijing. Despite Deng's seemingly open mind, the democracy wall was soon closed, and certain journals were shut down. Still, Deng knew that China needed Western technology and investment if the country was going to participate in the world economy. In December 1978, Deng announced a new "open door" policy, and on January 1, 1979, he launched full diplomatic relations with the United States. In so doing, the first whiffs of Western capitalism spread across urban China.

On his solitary day in Beijing, McGovern wandered around the city and looked into bookstores where people were lined up three deep to browse through the literature. "This is a publisher's dream," he thought. "I've got to get involved here as soon as I can." He hadn't seen a lot, but he'd seen enough to spark his plan. Realizing the difficulties he'd encounter trying to initiate a China venture, he stayed mum on his plans, even to IDG's board and executives. Conventional leadership wisdom suggests getting everyone on board early for most successful initiatives. But McGovern foresaw an opportunity that required early and unquestioned effort, so he forged ahead on his own.

In March 1980, McGovern made good on his promise to return. Without telling anyone at IDG and with no obvious path to setting up an IDG venture, he organized a technical seminar in Beijing and invited speakers from Microsoft and other tech companies. At the seminar, he met the Minister of the Computer and Electronics Industry and sat down to talk. Fully expecting a protracted negotiation, he was surprised when the minister said, "We need to inform our people about the information economy and the information age. Your information service would be very helpful to our growth. We would like to form a joint venture with you and make a weekly newspaper."

As always in life, timing was everything. Deng's decision to ease restrictions on foreign business in China gave McGovern the opening he needed—an opening that would not be available later. China banned the foreign ownership of newspapers after the 1989 Tiananmen Square incident. But by then, IDG was already entrenched and highly successful, and because its businesses were joint ventures with government ministries, it was allowed to continue its operations. IDG's publications were apolitical, so the Chinese officials overseeing the approvals for IDG felt there was no threat to their tightly controlled news flow. And as the minister had told McGovern, the government had focused a sharp eye on the potential of computers and technology for its emerging global economy, and IDG was the perfect outsider to be invited in.

In just three days, McGovern had ironed out the terms and conditions of a joint venture with the ministry that would result in the launch of a weekly newspaper called *China Computerworld*. He agreed to invest $250,000 to get the project rolling. Excited, McGovern went back to his hotel, typed up a press release announcing the deal, and slipped it under the door of the Beijing bureau of the *Wall Street Journal*. The "bureau" was a room in one of the Beijing hotels, and McGovern figured the newspaper would ignore this mysterious note. Instead, the *Journal* published a small article in the paper's US edition with the headline "First joint venture launched between the U.S. and China" or something along those lines.

When they read the paper the following day, the stunned IDG board members were not amused. Upon his return, McGovern was blasted with their fury. "What are you doing making deals with those commies?" they admonished. "You're going to ruin our brand. You can't do things like this without getting board approval! And if you had asked, we would have denied it."

Believing in the adage "It's easier to beg for forgiveness than ask for permission," McGovern eventually convinced the board of his vision for this prospective market. He had good reason to be optimistic. The ministry got all the required approvals in short order, and when the first issue of *China Computerworld* came out in October 1980, it was announced on state-run television. Within two weeks, there were 25,000 paid subscribers.

In a 1995 *Washington Post* article about IDG's China operations, McGovern boasted of IDG's success in the market. After 15 years, *China Computerworld* had higher revenues than any other Chinese publication, including the Communist Party's newspaper, *People's Daily*. At that point, IDG was publishing 12 computer newspapers and magazines in China with annual revenues of more than $40 million, a number that had risen 65 percent annually since McGovern first arrived. The combined circulation of those publications was 1.2 million, with a total monthly readership of over 18 million.[3]

First issue of *China Computerworld*, October 1980.

Pat signs agreement with China's minister of the computer and electronics industry.

China Computerworld, along with other IDG publications, owned a virtual monopoly on technology publishing in China. Its influence was widespread. "I simply can't make any business decision without reading *China Computerworld*," Liu Chuanzhi, then president of Legend Group, China's largest computer manufacturer, told the *Post*.

At a Beijing gathering of four original *China Computerworld* employees in 2017, the feeling of pride in what they had created was matched only by the palpable admiration they felt for McGovern. The group recalled how the initial effort was launched and how closely McGovern monitored the situation. "We knew Pat was a millionaire," said Tang Baoxing, one of *China Computerworld*'s first editors. "To us, he was this very rich person, but when he came to our office, he was just an ordinary person. He was kind and respectful; he shook hands with everybody." Such humility resonated throughout the nascent organization.

McGovern brought different IDG managers and editors to China to set up a de facto publishing class in order to teach the fledgling staff how to put out a weekly newspaper. As the publication began to get its bearings, he held the staff to the same exacting standards as any of his other global publications. "Every time Pat visited, he said 'You must grow your business.' He'd ask why our growth rate was so low and always push us to grow higher," Baoxing said. McGovern made sure the staff had the resources and office space it required, and he exhorted them to build on their success and launch other publications.

At its peak, *China Computerworld* ran over 10,000 pages of advertising each year and had more than two million readers. Individual issues were often more than 250 pages, which made it too big to be shipped on the trains that carried other Chinese newspapers. IDG launched 40 publications over the years, and because of its first-mover status, it developed the largest publishing infrastructure in China. *China Computerworld* had 300 employees, a significant size for a foreign company. Other Western publishers had to come to IDG for entrée into the market. IDG, through joint agreements with such publishers as Hearst and Condé Nast, published consumer magazines such as *Cosmopolitan, Esquire,* and *National Geographic* in China. McGovern liked to point out that IDG's initial $250,000 investment turned into $85 million in profit for IDG.

He had often heard the laughter at his naiveté and the comments that his global efforts were crazy and doomed to failure. Such negativity just spurred him on, and China was the crown jewel of his efforts. If nothing else, it confirmed that his gut feelings about prospective markets were sound and effective. Not every venture in every geography panned out, but most did, and McGovern came to believe that first movers in nascent markets had a huge advantage. IDG certainly did in China.

From all this, McGovern's leadership skills were sharpened to a fine edge. He had taken significant risks, and they had paid off. Risk, he realized, was heavily mitigated if a leader was willing to put in the time and travel to handle the due diligence that most executives delegate to others. When Deng Xiaoping died in 1997, McGovern published an op-ed tribute to him in the *New York Times.* In it, he noted his sense of a kindred spirit in Deng, a lingering feeling "that Deng understood me and grasped the needs of businesses like mine." He offered the view of someone who had come to understand that a successful business leader needs to have his feet on the ground if he intends to go global.

"Americans had warned me that the Chinese bureaucracy was impossible," he wrote. "Incredibly, though, six months after I arrived in China, we were open for business in a new building. Ignoring the conventional wisdom might have been one of the wisest decisions in my life. Today our flagship publication, *China Computerworld,* has almost 113,000 subscribers and the typical weekly issue runs 256 pages in six or seven sections, all sealed in a plastic bag as an advertising medium. . . .

"My first trip to China was followed by more than 50 others, all of which have allowed me to track the misinterpretation of Chinese affairs by those who impose American notions of freedom of expression on an Asian society. My experience has been different. I find ordinary citizens happier every time I visit. They know their standard of living is improving and they know that one man at the top set the transformation into motion. Modern China really works."[4]

VENTURE IN CHINA

McGovern's enchantment with China might have been tinged by a bit of naiveté. Modern China has indeed emerged as the world's second largest economy and is steadily growing toward the top spot. But China has many daunting issues—poverty, pollution, and inequality—that continue to plague the nation. Nonetheless, by the end of his life, McGovern had made more than 130 trips to China and was so beloved by the Chinese business community that he was considered an honorary citizen, and he was bestowed awards and honors no Westerner had ever won before. IDG China employees called him *Lao Mai*, a respectful paternal nickname that means Wise Elder.

Run by local publishers, editors, and journalists, IDG grew its publishing business into a $200-million-a-year juggernaut. McGovern believed deeply that his efforts in China were not only good for IDG but that the spread of knowledge about computers and information technology would serve to improve conditions for the Chinese people. It would also spur improvements in global relations between China and the rest of the world. As he became more familiar with the country, McGovern began to notice that many young Chinese students who had gone to the United States to get their college degrees were returning home to start businesses. The economy was roaring to life, and in 1993, he launched an even more audacious effort, IDG Venture Capital China, that country's first venture capital fund.

With his young protégé Hugo Shong and Shong's college friend Quan Zhou setting the course, McGovern once again followed a vision at which others scoffed. "Everyone would laugh at us," he said. "They said, 'There are no stock markets, no stock available in the company. You can't give stock options.'"

But McGovern had met with top Chinese leaders including then Chinese president Jiang Zemin, who told him they intended to build not just a manufacturing society but an innovation society. They wanted to create their own products: invent them, make them, and ship them, so that they got 85 percent of the selling price rather than the 12 percent they were getting at the time. "They told me, 'We're going to have stock markets, stock, entrepreneurs, just like in the US.' And we believed them," McGovern said. If nothing else, the venture fund would give IDG a vehicle for recycling its profits from its publishing business in China.

Hugo Shong was a Chinese journalist who had graduated from Boston University's College of Communication and was working as a reporter for a Cahners technology magazine in Boston. Shong was ambitious and a quick learner. As a young man in China, he had worked as an electrician in a factory, making $6 a month. Having lived through Mao's infamous Cultural Revolution from 1966 to 1976, he understood clearly the opportunity that was suddenly in front of him.

While Shong was a student at the Fletcher School of Law and Diplomacy at Tufts University, a chance meeting with McGovern in 1988 at a business dinner made him aware of this dynamic publishing magnate. On the advice of his friend Quan, who had a PhD in fiber optics from Rutgers, Shong wrote a letter to McGovern asking for an interview. To his surprise, McGovern's assistant, Mary Dolaher, called and set up a one-hour meeting. The meeting lasted three hours, and McGovern, seeking new blood for his Chinese publishing operations, saw something special in Shong.

He hired Shong immediately and mentored him for three years at IDG's headquarters in the United States. By 1992, Shong became McGovern's key executive in China, building the publishing business and eventually launching the IDG venture capital fund.

McGovern initially tasked Shong with finding someone to spearhead the venture capital effort, but it proved to be a difficult hire. Talented Silicon Valley venture capitalists did not speak the language and had little interest in relocating to China. Stephen Coit, a partner at Charles River Ventures and member of IDG's board, came to Beijing and met with Shong. When he returned to the United States, Coit told McGovern that Shong was the only person who had the passion required to initiate the new venture. Though Shong had no venture capital experience, Coit believed he could learn quickly, and McGovern agreed. Suddenly, the young former journalist was leading a technology investment firm.

Shong was prescient enough to hire Quan Zhou to help him set up the fund. Quan was a brilliant engineer who had won awards from NASA and held a US patent in fiber optic devices. His technical savvy and intuition would bring much-needed wisdom to the new venture effort. The pair became pioneers and built what would become China's most successful venture capital firm. "People said that China was ten years too early to do venture," Shong recalled. "But Pat believed in me."

In 1993, IDG established its first venture fund with a $20 million investment in a joint venture with the Science and Technology Commission of Shanghai Municipality. Shong and Quan met with a steady flow of smart and ambitious entrepreneurs and invested small amounts—$300,000 to $500,000—in several startups. If something seemed particularly impressive, the investment would be higher. But starting a venture capital effort from scratch in an emerging economy required enormous patience. As Shong recalled, "For the first seven years, there was no return. We worried every time Pat visited, usually five or six times a year, that he would be disappointed and withdraw his investment. That never happened. He always remained optimistic and encouraged us to carry on our work."

Finally, in 2000, many of the early fund investments had initial public offerings and money started pouring in, even as tech stocks slumped in the United States. For example, IDG invested $1.2 million in a company called Tencent, which it later sold for $200 million. Tencent went on to become the world's largest instant messaging company. Shong didn't want to sell so early, but McGovern and some of IDG's financial people insisted. Shong is painfully aware that the investment eventually would have been worth billions. Another significant investment of $2 million in Baidu, China's largest search engine provider, returned $700 million. Eventually, venture capital spawned 70 percent of IDG's profits.

Charles Zhang, founder of Sohu, a popular Chinese search engine, was an early Internet entrepreneur. With a PhD in physics from MIT, he foresaw an opportunity in the early 1990s when the Internet was in its early stages in the United States and barely existent in China. Zhang left MIT and returned to China in 1996 with seed money from two MIT professors. He founded Sohu in 1998, and a chance meeting on an airplane with Quan lead to an investment by IDG. Zhang became a wealthy rock star in China with Sohu's early success, and he attributes McGovern's venture capital achievement in China to creative thinking.

"Success in venture capital is in trusting the right people, like Hugo and Quan, and letting them do their thing," Zhang said. "None of the big Silicon Valley firms succeeded here because they treated China like a branch office. They didn't have the kind of drive that was required. IDG works like an entrepreneurial company in China. Pat himself was an entrepreneur, so he understood what it required. That's why IDG became the Kleiner Perkins of China."

McGovern traveled extensively in China, and throughout these visits, he sought opportunities that others had not yet discovered. He established strong ties in the city of Shenzhen, which he envisioned as a technology center and an ideal location for venture capital investing. In 1998, IDG signed an agreement to invest 1 billion yuan (around $125 million) over 10 years in Shenzhen. In just a couple of years, IDG had invested in 20 start-ups in the city, and McGovern was given the title "Honorable Citizen of Shenzhen." Later, he received the International Investment Achievement Award from CCTV, something no foreigner had ever gotten. With his influence, Shenzhen grew into a hotbed of technology innovation and development.

Pat McGovern with his International Investment Achievement Award
from CCTV in China, an award no foreigner had ever received.

Having first-mover status in China's fledgling venture capital market, IDG attracted a growing amount of attention from venture firms in Silicon Valley. In 2005, McGovern agreed to a joint venture in China with Jim Breyer, a partner at Accel Partners and a longtime acquaintance of McGovern. Breyer, one of venture capital's superstar investors, pointed out one of the lessons he learned from McGovern about succeeding in China.

"Pat walked the walk when it came to long-term investing and thinking in a way that is extraordinarily rare," Breyer said. Venture capitalists are by nature impatient and eager for returns on their investments. But McGovern knew instinctively that China was a market where introspection and patient consideration mattered.

"I learned a great deal from Pat about his long-term intuition and passion for taking a 10- to 20-year view," Breyer said. For McGovern, it was not just the 10-plus years of the investment but also the building of relationships and commitments that were extraordinarily long-term and crucial to doing business. Breyer, who now runs his own venture firm, Breyer Capital, still partners with IDG in China. In fact, in 2016 he announced a new $1 billion fund in partnership with IDG Capital.

The venture business in China was so successful, dovetailing nicely with the US-based venture fund, that IDG decided to set up similar firms in South Korea, India, and Vietnam. McGovern identified dynamic individuals such as Sudhir Sethi in India and Henry Nguyen in Vietnam and invested in their initial funds.

Nguyen, a Harvard-educated Vietnamese American, was mentored by both Quan Zhou and Coit as he set up Vietnam's first and largest venture fund in 2005. Jeffrey Bussgang, who teaches entrepreneurship at Harvard Business School and is a general partner at Flybridge Capital Partners in Boston, authored a book in 2010 called *Mastering the VC Game* in which he profiled Nguyen. He said Nguyen is considered "the John Doerr of Vietnam," referencing the famed Silicon Valley venture capitalist, and was running IDG's Vietnamese fund by age 30.

"When Henry Nguyen started in Vietnam, there was no word or phrase that described venture capital," Bussgang wrote. "So he had to develop one. 'The term we chose translates directly to "risk growth capital."'" Nguyen told Bussgang. "'We wanted to make the point that we're not risk takers. We're not guys who are jumping out of airplanes. It's a risk because, hey, these are very young businesses that are trying to do novel things and the odds of success are against them.'"[5]

McGovern's decision to invest $150 million in Sudhir Sethi's first Indian venture fund in 2006 was a game changer. "We shared a lot with him," Sethi recalled about his encounters with McGovern. "We knew he had global experience and, very important, business and revenue models. His choice of tech investments was where no man had gone before. From him, we learned how to handle risk and how to pick the best entrepreneurs." Always believing that IDG was a family of companies designed to help and support each other, McGovern put Sethi in touch with the partners in the China, Vietnam, and US venture funds to provide much-needed guidance and mentoring.

BEYOND CAMBRIDGE

McGovern's passion for spreading the gospel of IT and his budding embrace of venture capital was equally matched by his obsession for championing research on the human brain. When he and his wife, Lore, pledged $350 million to MIT in 2000 for the creation of the McGovern Institute for Brain Research, it was in their plans to eventually build such research centers in other parts of the world, including China.

Soon after the MIBR moved into its shining new headquarters in Kendall Square in Cambridge, the McGoverns went to China to establish a similar center. McGovern suggested they follow the same process they had employed to identify the perfect home for the institute in the United States, so a few leading Chinese universities were invited to submit proposals. Neuroscience research in China was not nearly at the same level as in America, so the invitation spawned an enthusiastic response from a number of universities eager to connect with McGovern.

In fact, Hong Bo, an associate dean at Tsinghua, read an article in 2006 about McGovern in which he spoke about his plans to set up an institute in China. Hong sent the article along with a note to Tsinghua's president Chen Xi, a close friend and college roommate of Chinese president Xi Jinping, suggesting the university reach out to McGovern and invite him to a meeting. McGovern was treated to demonstrations of some of the school's neuroscience research and was duly impressed. By 2008, Hong had met with Robert Desimone, director of the MIBR, and set up an academic exchange between Tsinghua and MIT to try to encourage graduate students and faculty to communicate and collaborate on their research. McGovern wanted to hear from other universities as well, though he was clearly taken with the Tsinghua pitch.

In 2009, McGovern met with Dong Qi, president of Beijing Normal University, who invited him to tour the campus and see the neuroscience research group. Dong was amazed at McGovern's understanding of the research and realized this successful businessman was just as devoted to brain research as he was to his companies.

"We talked about our research into children's learning, language, math, music, sports skills. He thought this was a very important area," Dong said. "China has a huge population of children, and if we understand more about their brain development, their learning disabilities, and the brain function, this will be a great help to us and to children all over the world."

Amid these visits and conversations, something intriguing was stirring within China's academic and research institutions. After decades of losing its best and brightest science and engineering talent to the United States, an increasing number of leading Chinese researchers were returning from prestigious academic posts in the United States, drawn by a surge in financial resources, promises to build state-of-the-art research facilities, and a strong sense of national pride.

Among those returning was Dr. Shi Yigong, a top molecular biologist who had rejected a $10 million grant at Princeton University, where he was a full professor, to return to Tsinghua in China in 2008. These repatriated scientists were well aware of McGovern, the MIBR, and the opportunity to get in on the ground floor of a new brain research institute.

Proposals came from Tsinghua, Peking University, and Beijing Normal University, all leading educational institutions with strong science credentials. The competition grew fierce, and while one university promised to match the McGovern grant dollar for dollar, one-to-one, others upped the ante and offered to match two-for-one and even three-for-one. Still, Tsinghua, which has been called the MIT of China, had the inside track. Dr. Shi had dinner with

McGovern and impressed him with his low-key but enlightening description of the work and potential at Tsinghua. "I could tell from his body language that he was going to choose Tsinghua," Dr. Shi said. According to Desimone, an advisor on the selection, all the proposals were strong.

The McGoverns planned to give a $3 million annual grant for 10 years to the winner. After visiting all the institutions, they chose Tsinghua. As they were leaving Tsinghua with a verbal handshake agreement, the McGoverns, Desimone, and Hugo Shong were in a car heading back to the hotel when Shong received a call on his cell phone. "We've been asked to meet with Madame Liu Yandong," he told the group. At the time, Madame Liu was a key government figure in the area of science and education (today Liu is a high-ranking vice premier of China), and she wanted to meet the McGoverns at a secure government enclave near the Forbidden City.

The room was set up in a formal Chinese manner, with assigned seats for everyone, and pictures were taken. "It was clear she was influenced to give us a message," Desimone recalled. "And the message was yes, Tsinghua is a great place for the institute, but we should really consider Beijing Normal University."

Liu was impressive. She talked knowledgeably about McGovern and IDG without notes for 30 minutes. The message was indeed clear: it would be far better to fund more than one institute in China. Few foreigners understood the subtleties of doing business in China as well as McGovern. Though he never intended to divide his donation in this manner, it was clear to him how this had to proceed. So in 2011, McGovern formally announced the creation of brain research institutes at Tsinghua, Beijing Normal, and Peking University. Each would receive $1 million a year, and though each would be a separate research institute, they would cooperate and share resources and research.

It was an unorthodox and unplanned solution, but in the end, "it worked out really well," Desimone said. "The impact was bigger because it was across the three universities." In 2011, the doors to the McGovern Institutes for Brain Research at three universities were officially opened. Though the actual dollar amount is not staggering, the funding is crucial.

"We get lots of government funding," said Rao Yi of Peking University. "But it is heavily regulated, so it is not always able to be used the most effectively. That's why the philanthropy really helps us, because that's where we can put it in the niches we really need and make it work."

A SILK ROAD

IDG would eventually do business in nearly 100 countries, and McGovern took personal pride in every one of those operations. But China remained especially close to his heart because he had dared to be audacious, step off a plane without a visa or a friend in Beijing, and forge a path along his own personal Silk Road.

For Eugene Yu, a former assistant of political affairs for the Chinese ambassador to the United States, McGovern was among the most influential foreigners to come to China. Yu, who eventually came to work for IDG in China and served as McGovern's interpreter on many visits, said McGovern's contributions to China were widespread and vital.

By creating the technology publishing business in China, McGovern was a catalyst for China to develop its own information technology business. "With these publications, people began to realize what was going on around the world," Yu said. "Before that, China was very ignorant about what was happening in the IT area."

With the joint agreements with publishers like Hearst and Condé Nast, Chinese readers had access to a wide range of lifestyle magazines. Suddenly, the Chinese people, with a burgeoning middle class, were thinking about lifestyle issues in a way they never had before.

On the venture capital front, IDG's pioneering efforts helped convince Chinese students studying abroad to come back to China because suddenly there was money, a new market, and a future for them in China.

By bringing the brain research institute to three Chinese universities, McGovern provided the leadership that helped awaken the Chinese government and research institutions to the idea that brain research could be a huge boon for China.

"His impact lasted more than 30 years," Yu said. "He educated China in so many different ways, and it was Pat who made so much difference in the way people work, think, and live."

TAKEAWAYS

▶▶ Identify new markets before the rest of the world gets wind of the potential.

▶▶ Get on a plane and put your feet on the ground in uncharted territory. It is the only way to effectively find these early opportunities.

▶▶ Use joint ventures and deals with government ministries, if necessary, to gain a foothold in emerging markets. First-mover efforts usually pay off.

▶▶ In a challenging market such as China, cultivate a trusted local executive who understands the culture, speaks the language, and can lead a difficult journey to a fruitful payoff.

▶▶ Spend more time listening than talking. It is a key sign of respect that will pay huge dividends.

LESSON THREE
Decentralize: When Building a Global Empire, Every Market Is Local

Every tub on its own bottom.
—JOHN BUNYAN,
in *Pilgrim's Progress*, 1678

IDG's success was built on a long list of innovative achievements, but the company became known and admired for Pat McGovern's singular devotion to a radical decentralized management structure.

From its earliest efforts to expand into new markets and new geographies, IDG followed a strict formula that gave nearly autonomous control to each business unit, regardless of where it was located. The power lay in the hands of each business unit manager or country manager who could operate independently as long as the managers made their numbers. The lean headquarters staff would remain at a distance, and McGovern would steadfastly support this global self-rule.

Ironically, McGovern's decision to build a decentralized organization was born more from pragmatism than management
wisdom. As a young entrepreneur, he was determined to make
sure that everything in his new venture ran smoothly, and that he
retained complete control of the fledgling organization.

"I would want to approve any major new financial commitment," he recalled in an interview years later. "I would want to
meet all the key people being hired by the company. I always loved
to be in touch with the customers, so I would constantly be traveling. I would travel for 10 days or two weeks, and when I would
come back, I would see a big stack of things in my basket. I remember one evening thinking, 'Oh my God, I'm slowing the growth of
this company rather than accelerating it.' I said, 'Well, what does it
really take to make a successful business?'"

His epiphany came when he realized that there had been "tens
of thousands of very successful companies that had survived quite
well without input and advice from Patrick McGovern." As the central authority, he was holding back the progress of IDG, and that
just wouldn't do, especially for a corporate strategy that focused on
global expansion.

"What is really the basis of success?" he asked himself. "The
first thing is to find a fertile market, find a need out there that you
can fulfill at a cost that is less than perceived value, so you can
make a little profit off a positive cash flow and have a healthy business. Then you have to find someone who is passionate and inspired
by the opportunity to fulfill that need, someone whose passion and
energy and enthusiasm attracts others to join them, and they can
provide leadership to them.

"Then you have to support that person the way you would like
to be supported in their position. You want to have trust in them,
and you want to encourage them. You want to celebrate their successes. You want to give them the resources they ask for. You want
to get out of their way and let them do it the way they think is right,
and let them listen to the marketplace and the customers and let
that be the guiding force rather than looking over their shoulder

and telling them what your opinion is, because you are not the customer."

As the company entered the 1970s, IDG became a decentralized organization in the true sense of the word, and the company's fortunes took off. Decentralized management was more than a business structure—it was a corporate philosophy that later, decades after McGovern infused such thinking into IDG's DNA, was perfectly captured by the popular saying, "Think global, act local." Only a man who had put his wingtips on the ground in well over 100 countries and took the time in those places to learn the culture and meet the people could truly understand what "local" meant. Among the lessons he preached: "If we can't globalize it, why are we doing it? It is better to be early into important markets; too early is less bad than too late."

McGovern believed that the business unit manager closest to the customer and the marketplace should be making the final decisions. The local experts understood the markets, the customers, and the employees in those markets, and ultimately, this would maximize the value of IDG brands in those markets.

Reflecting on those early days, McGovern explained his thinking. "I really changed the whole philosophy of our business at that point saying, 'Every new project, we're going to treat it as a new business. We'll launch a new company and hire a CEO, and tell that person that they are really the CEO. We will form a board of directors for that company, so that person won't have to report to a boss. They would report to the board like any other true CEO.'"

Headquarters' role was one of support and fiscal reality checks. If business unit managers made their numbers, they rarely saw or heard from McGovern. In fact, McGovern sublimated the IDG brand in favor of visibility for the individual publications, so that each business unit could promote its own brand to the world. Readers identified with *Computerworld* or *PCWorld* or *InfoWorld*, rather than with IDG, much the same way consumers were loyal to Crest or Tide, rather than Procter & Gamble.

Decentralization eventually gained popularity in the 1980s and beyond, with business school professors touting its advantages and leaders such as Warren Buffett speaking about its virtues.

"[Decentralization] produces an occasional major mistake that might have been eliminated or minimized through closer operating controls," Buffett wrote in his 1979 letter to shareholders of Berkshire Hathaway. "But it also eliminates large layers of costs and dramatically speeds decision-making. Because everyone has a great deal to do, a very great deal gets done."[1]

"There is a fundamental humility to decentralization, an admission that headquarters does not have all the answers and that much of the real value is created by local managers in the field," added William N. Thorndike Jr., managing director of Housatonic Partners, a Boston-based investment firm, in his book *The Outsiders.*[2]

In today's digitally connected, hypercompetitive, globalized business environment, decentralization is no longer an outlier, but when McGovern championed it, it was considered innovative and radical. "People thought he was crazy when he first did it," said Pat Kenealy, the former CEO of IDG. "Now everybody does it, but he was doing this 20 years earlier than other people."

York von Heimburg, president, International IDG Communications, agreed. "In 1960s business in the U.S., the focus was on the need to be big; size was all," von Heimburg said. "They had the need to cover the world with one company, driven from the U.S. Pat did the exact opposite. At that time, to build a global company with a decentralized structure with the belief that business is local, information is local, customer relationships are local; that was absolutely revolutionary."

A LEADER WITHOUT BORDERS

In 1968, McGovern was invited to Japan to give a talk about how information technology would improve society in the twenty-first century. There, McGovern was introduced to Dempa Publications, a large Japanese publishing company that was interested in doing a weekly publication like *Computerworld*. Intrigued, McGovern offered to be a partner in a joint venture, but the Japanese took an extraordinarily long time to make the decision to follow through. They were extremely detail-oriented and sent a team to the United States. Over the course of three weeks at the *Computerworld* office in Newton, Japanese editors and production people observed each job function and took pictures and copious notes. The idea was to mimic everything the staff did in the United States.

McGovern was impatient but stayed the course. Dempa was Japan's leading publisher focused on information services and electronics, and for McGovern, Japan represented a fertile market with unlimited upside. The joint venture finally bore fruit in May 1973, when *Computerworld* announced the maiden issue of its sister publication *Shukan Computer*, which means *Computer Weekly* in Japanese. *Shukan Computer* started with a circulation of 35,000. Japan's Ministry of International Trade and Industry projected that by 1975, the country would have 38,000 computers worth more than $12 billion. For IDG, planting a flag there seemed to be a promising first step toward globalization. But according to Walter Boyd, *Computerworld's* managing editor who became McGovern's trusted right-hand man at IDG, this initial international foray was more frustrating than rewarding. Sometimes letting local managers have full control didn't work, especially if there was a fundamental difference in goals and expected outcomes.

"They never got what Pat wanted to get done," Boyd recalled. "We kept that relationship going for seven years, and we lost a lot of ground in Japan, which we never regained. We would go to board meetings there every year on Thanksgiving, and we'd spend the whole day telling them to do this or that, and they would say, 'You don't understand Japanese culture' and revert back to what they had been doing."

Eventually, IDG bought out Dempa and took 100 percent control of the publication. The lesson was vivid. Decentralization would succeed or fail based on giving the business unit full control. Expecting a clone of the original *Computerworld* would be frustrating and ultimately fruitless. Undaunted, McGovern turned his sights on Brazil, and later the United Kingdom, France, and Germany. In its global march, IDG used wholly owned subsidiaries, joint ventures, and license deals to set up shop in new geographies. McGovern didn't care for joint ventures; he wanted total control, but in some venues, such as communist countries, he had no choice. Decentralization was most effective when IDG had a wholly owned subsidiary.

At the outset, McGovern would visit these countries, identify an individual with the requisite skills to launch and lead the new effort, and give this person the resources to get started. Eager to move quickly, McGovern sometimes chose the right geography but the wrong entrepreneur to run it. His intuition would occasionally fail him, and the person he tapped for the top spot simply didn't have the needed skill set or leadership qualities to run a business unit.

"When we started, Pat would go in and hire somebody, and Bill Murphy (IDG's longtime CFO) and I would go in later and straighten it out," Boyd said. "Quite often, that person would hire good people, but the guy in charge wasn't right and needed to be replaced."

McGovern never wavered in his belief in decentralization, both domestically, where IDG's publishing, research, and trade show efforts were rapidly expanding into burgeoning new technology markets, and internationally, where the thirst for knowledge about information technology was insatiable.

Even as the Japanese joint venture struggled, McGovern was already planting the IDG flag in Germany, where *Computerwoche*, the German *Computerworld*, commenced publication in 1974. Realizing that Germany was Europe's largest electronic data processing market, McGovern wanted to expand. In 1978, Boyd encountered Eckhard Utpadel, a marketing whiz born in East Germany. Smart, quirky, and self-assured, Utpadel was the kind of manager Boyd believed to be especially suited for a role with

Celebrating *Computerwoche*'s twentieth birthday with
Dieter Eckbauer, the German publication's editor in chief.

IDG. Boyd introduced Utpadel to McGovern, and the two hit it off immediately.

"From the beginning, Pat wanted to create a publishing opportunity for people who were cut off, especially in the Eastern bloc," Utpadel recalled. "That got me totally. He said, 'Eckhard, come on. We'll do it. We'll conquer the world.'"

For McGovern, who as a recent college graduate in 1960 had been arrested by Soviet police in a park near the Kremlin for trying to share information about Western democracy, the Cold War provided a siren call to action. He envisioned computer publications in all of the Eastern bloc nations, including the Soviet Union, and in Utpadel, he found a willing partner.

"To bring information to the people who were cut off because of politics, it was a key message for me," Utpadel said. "If people get the information and are informed, they'll not make war."

Utpadel became publisher and managing director of *Computerwoche* and took on ever-expanding responsibilities for IDG in Europe. He was joined by a growing roster of talented young managers intent on building IDG's presence around the world. Every year, a new publication was established in a new country, starting with Czechoslovakia and followed by Poland, Romania, Bulgaria, and Hungary. At the same time, IDG was expanding across Western Europe and Scandinavia, as well as South America.

In the early 1980s, McGovern turned to Axel Leblois, the dynamic young executive he had hired in France, and told him, "We should open up Eastern Europe." Leblois was impressed. "He was a leader without borders," Leblois said of McGovern. "Nothing would limit IDG's outreach."

When McGovern set his sights on countries behind the Iron Curtain in the mid-1980s, he counseled Leblois on how difficult it would be to set up shop in these geographies. McGovern suggested he look first at Hungary and find the telltale signs, signs McGovern had seen in Beijing in 1978, that would suggest great market potential. In Hungary's case, Leblois did some exploration and discovered a raft of software companies, PC makers, and a high concentration of bookstores, which is a good indicator of a market that would embrace new magazines. The intent was always to help wake up the information economy.

Hungary was a tech market waiting to be born, and IDG's foray was an immediate success. "We were profitable from day one," Leblois recalled. He hired a Hungarian publisher and editor and oversaw a joint venture with the Ministry of Planning. Echoing a mandate from McGovern, he made it clear that the local editors ran the show, and there could be no censorship from the government.

A year later, due to the success of this decentralized effort, the Hungarian minister sought Leblois's counsel on starting a stock market, a remarkable economic moment for this communist nation. That same year, McGovern brought Leblois to the United States to become president and CEO of CW Communications, a key part of IDG's publishing business.

As a global leader, McGovern "believed human nature was the same everywhere," Leblois added. "He was able to understand people and show empathy for them that created incredible loyalty to him. To empower people is the most important trigger for the whole decentralized system. There wouldn't be a story like IDG without decentralized management."

By the time Frank Cutitta joined IDG in 1984 to sell advertising abroad, the company had already established its reputation as an international powerhouse in the technology media business. But the push to globalize increased as the 1980s and the advent of personal computers, networks, and business software fueled a global technology revolution. Between 1984 and 2011, IDG's international publications soared from 15 to 295. Eventually, McGovern would be able to boast that IDG published on all of the earth's seven continents, including Antarctica. "During my history at IDG, we measured years in the number of gatefolds listing international publications in the corporate brochure," Cutitta explained. "When I joined, there was a single spread. When I left, there were eight gatefolds, and when somebody opened it, they inevitably said, 'Holy shit!'"

Cutitta and his boss David Hill spent 200,000 miles or more each year on airplanes, planting flags for McGovern. "He would come in with the name of a possible magazine from Budapest on a cocktail napkin and say, 'Go make that a publication,'" Cutitta said.

McGovern had a vision for world domination from the outset in 1964. "International wasn't something different," Cutitta said. "It was what we did. IDG was always genetically international because of him."

THE DOWNSIDE OF DECENTRALIZATION

Setting up subsidiaries and licensees in communist countries and unstable democracies was a daunting task. Deals had to be made with government ministries, and finding the individuals with the skill and integrity to run the operations was a constant challenge. McGovern's foray into China in 1980 had been met with skepticism and derision from pundits and industry analysts. Even the IDG board questioned his sanity. McGovern, a student of Eastern philosophy and a proverbial cockeyed optimist, believed to his core that people were people, regardless of the politics under which they lived, and this new erupting technology era would eventually strike a nerve with everyone on the planet. The desire for information about technology would fuel strong growth far into the future.

In the late 1980s, when McGovern decided it was time to enter the Soviet Union, the challenges were even greater than he had encountered when he set up shop in China. Though Russia and China had both been under communist regimes for a half-century or more, the Chinese never lost the sense of how to do business. The Russians, on the other hand, lost all touch with capitalism and had little insight into how business was done. This required a steep learning curve for outside ventures in Moscow.

The Soviets, after all, were historic Cold War enemies, and beyond the usual logistics of finding the right country manager and maneuvering around government entities, there were the many levels of paranoia associated with doing business in Russia. Perestroika and glasnost were fine in theory, but in reality, old methods and mistrusts died hard. Cutitta, who would end up spending significant time living and working in the Soviet Union, explained, "We had to convince people we weren't giving COBOL to the commies. Technology, for McGovern, was part of connecting the world."

McGovern also had a sixth sense about prospective markets and was intrigued about the difficulties of life behind the Iron Curtain. "He had a certain energy," said Cutitta, "In all those experiences, he had a good natural sense for cross-cultural issues. It was amazing watching him. If there was a misstep, it never threw him off the rails."

In 1988, when IDG heard that the Supreme Council at the Kremlin had declared that it would accept foreign investment, McGovern immediately flew to Moscow to set up shop. He met with the Academy of Sciences and the Printing and Publishing Ministry. News and information flow in the Soviet Union was so restrained that these people had not heard about the new decree. They said to come back in a few months after they looked into the new regulation. When McGovern went back with Cutitta, there was a clamoring to become IDG's partner in a joint venture. After maneuvering through the bureaucracy to find a viable partner, the first issue of *PCWorld USSR* was put together.

The agreement called for a first issue of 150 pages, with 120 editorial, 30 advertising. At a launch party at the National Hotel, which McGovern and several IDG leaders attended, the first issue was delivered, but amid the 150 pages, there were only four ads. After the party, McGovern went to the Moscow office and asked about the ads. "We got the ads," he was told, "but in our country, the editor in chief is in charge of everything in the publication. He read the ads and found half of them were boring. They didn't have enough technical content to be suitable to present to his readers."

McGovern tried to explain the concept of perestroika and that in a market economy, publications needed advertising to pay the bills. "If we don't get the advertising, we don't have any revenue and we can't pay the bills," he said. "We can't pay your salary. It's not good for your family." He finally convinced them that they had to include the advertising. For several years, the Russian experiment moved ahead in fits and starts.

David Hill, the head of IDG's international licensing and franchising efforts for 15 years, was on the front lines of the company's expansion. He spent much of his time on airplanes for the 28 years he worked at IDG, and he successfully set up license deals in 50 to 60 countries. "I thought this job would be pretty cool because I liked to travel," Hill said. "But my challenge became getting home."

The process of building the IDG empire put a bright spotlight on the highs and lows of decentralization. The concept drove IDG to become a multibillion-dollar international media powerhouse. But it came with the risk and reality of some dark and confounding moments.

"If you get really good, strong, entrepreneurial country managers around the world and you give them their head, they do great things," Hill explained. "But the downside is every few years, one of them is going to go south because you're not paying very much attention to them. And when one does, because we were so decentralized, you may not know about how bad things are going for a year or two. When you finally figure it out, there's a hell of a mess that's got to be cleaned up."

The first such mess emerged in Moscow, seemingly out of nowhere. In the midst of a 16-hour-long IDG management meeting in Boston in 1995, McGovern received a fax from Moscow. It was from Boris Antoniuk, IDG's partner in Moscow, who stated, "Pat, the company is now mine."

McGovern was stunned and angry. IDG's subsidiary in Moscow, which had been established as a joint venture to publish *PCWorld* in 1988, had a history of operating problems, so in 1991, when McGovern launched *Computerworld* in Russia, he decided to set it up as a separate entity from *PCWorld*. Hill, who arrived in February 1991, to help train the staff of the new *Computerworld*, found that the *PCWorld* operation was disorganized and poorly run. Here was an instance where the local management was not performing as required. Hill also noted that Antoniuk, a brilliant apparatchik with an extensive network inside the Kremlin, was involved in several other ventures and was not paying enough attention to *PCWorld*.

Keith Arnot, IDG's London-based international controller, recalled that his boss at the time, Ian Thalmessinger, went to Russia to meet with Antoniuk and his staff. A report was submitted, and it seemed that the situation was resolved. But several months later, when Antoniuk initiated his coup attempt, he complained that McGovern had not visited him in four months and "I feel like I am a satellite operation." He didn't appreciate being isolated in this manner, so he had set up a new office, taken the employees and the business activities, and declared, "You no longer have a business in Moscow."

McGovern summoned Thalmessinger and Hill and told them to get over to Moscow to confront Antoniuk and take back the company. "It became pretty clear that Russia was equivalent to the Wild West," Arnot recalled.

According to Thalmessinger, the first trip accomplished little but to underscore the magnitude and "virtual impossibility of recovering the company," given the lack of litigation procedures. "At the time, commercial disputes were simply settled out of court, with bullets, grenades, and explosives," Thalmessinger said.

But violence was not an option, so on a subsequent trip to Moscow, Thalmessinger hired a UK-based law firm with an office in Moscow to try to resolve the conflict.

"In the Russia of those days, the way you did it was you hired bigger, nastier, better connections than the other side had. And that's what we did," Hill said. Fighting fire with fire meant resorting to some strong-arm measures. Cutitta, with some extensive contacts in Moscow, joined Thalmessinger to try to find a resolution. He contacted Mikhail Volodarsky, who had been IDG's first country manager in 1988, and asked him to help. Volodarsky set up a meeting at Moscow's Radisson Slavyanskaya hotel and introduced them to a former KGB colonel who was the head of his own consulting firm, specializing in security and dispute resolution.

According to Thalmessinger, the consultant told him the process would take time and he would need a fee of $50,000, which Thalmessinger agreed to. The consultant then presented a list of the levels of destruction he could provide, including eliminating Antoniuk, his family, and others.

"My instant response to this was that we wanted exactly the opposite, namely that his mission was to make certain that no harm came to Boris or to any members of his family," Thalmessinger said. "His specific task was to recover the company without harming or injuring anybody. I think he thought we were completely nuts; that this wasn't the way business was conducted in Russia, but he eventually agreed to the condition."

The dispute went on for several weeks, and McGovern grew more anxious, asking for regular progress reports. McGovern was deeply invested in the Russia subsidiary, both financially and emotionally. He believed there was a potentially lucrative market there, similar to China and the Eastern bloc nations. When he felt threatened in this manner, he did not take it lightly. When things felt like they had reached a stalemate, he lashed out at Thalmessinger and said, "Look, if you can't do it, then I'll find someone who will."

The outburst, uncharacteristic of the usually even-tempered McGovern, underscored his frustration with the Moscow situation. "Pat had a predefined way of doing things, and he would follow that relentlessly," Arnot said. "He was tenacious." Though McGovern would never have sanctioned doing anything potentially threatening or outside the law, he also felt clear "that this can't happen and we're going to reverse it." Once someone had spent time working at IDG, McGovern felt they had joined the family, and he had difficulty embracing the fact that such a manager might generate a crisis.

"Pat would treat his country managers as his children," Arnot said, "and he would always regard each country manager as being king of the country."

The final meeting to resolve the matter was held in Antoniuk's office along with the former KGB colonel. Volodarsky remained outside, waiting in the car. Thalmessinger spoke no Russian, but he understood that Antoniuk was ready to quit his coup attempt and promptly return the joint venture company to IDG. He told Thalmessinger he was surprised that IDG had gone to such lengths to take back the venture since he didn't think McGovern was particularly interested in what was happening in Russia.

The security consultant informed Thalmessinger that because the effort had taken far longer than originally anticipated and was far more difficult to resolve in this restrained manner, he would need a much higher fee. "The clear implication was that it would be unwise for me to attempt to leave Moscow before the amount was settled," Thalmessinger said.

Though rare, when trouble occurred, IDG headquarters could move quickly. Arnot recounted a frantic call he received on a Friday afternoon from Thalmessinger. "Ian said, 'I need you to arrange a transfer of $50,000 to a bank account in Guernsey,'" Arnot said, referring to the Guernsey Channel Islands, which are known for being a tax haven. Arnot asked him why, and Thalmessinger responded, "I'm in trouble. The people I'm in contact with have told me that if I don't pay this money, and if the money isn't in that bank account by the weekend, I'm not going to get out of the country."

So spooked was Thalmessinger that on his last night in Moscow, he changed rooms at the hotel three times. He used pillows to create a dummy in the bed and slept in the bathtub, figuring it offered him greater protection. "It was one of my worst nights ever," he recalled. Fortunately, the night passed quietly.

Arnot contacted Ted Bloom, IDG's chief financial officer, and the money was transferred. The crisis was over. To his regret, Antoniuk learned that it was a bad idea to try to cheat McGovern. Shortly after the debacle ended, IDG turned the subsidiary into a licensing deal and Antoniuk was left out in the cold.

FROM THE FRYING PAN

Feeling like he was becoming a character in a John le Carré novel, Hill was called in yet again in 1998 when trouble flared up in IDG's subsidiary in Turkey. Running the subsidiary was a man named Mehmet Ali Altaca who called McGovern one morning and declared in a panic, "I've got a serious problem. If I don't have a million dollars by Friday, they're going to take everything!"

Unable to discern who was behind this nefarious plot, McGovern had no intention of sending a million dollars. Instead, he called Hill, who was in Dubai at the time, and Kevin Krull, IDG's chief counsel, and told them to head to Istanbul to resolve the crisis. "We were warned that it was a very ugly situation," Hill recalled.

After meeting with lawyers to sort out the situation, Hill and Krull learned that Ali Altaca had launched several ill-advised business activities, such as trade shows and marginal publications. When IDG refused to send money to fund these ventures, he started borrowing money at an average interest rate of 117 percent. The interest payments alone were more than twice the profits of the company, and many suppliers had not been paid. When one supplier cut him off, he found another. He convinced members of his staff to take out personal loans and then turn the money over to the company. And he told everyone, from employees to the banks to the suppliers, that IDG would take care of them.

Given the circumstances, Hill and Krull enlisted the aid of Demitrij Halkov, a Czech security consultant who used to work for "the other side" during the Communist era. When they arrived in Istanbul, they quickly learned that Ali Altaca had also been borrowing from some unsavory sources and telling them that IDG was good for the money.

When Krull and Hill arrived at IDG's Istanbul office on a Monday morning, the office was completely empty. No tables, chairs, file cabinets, or computers. The pair, with Halkov watching their backs, stayed in Istanbul for a week, trying to sort out the chaos. "Everybody was after us," Hill said. "Once people found out that we were in the country, they started trying to get to us, figuring they could squeeze some money out of us."

On the last night in the city, Hill got a call in the middle of the night from Halkov telling him to pack his bags and be in the hallway in 10 minutes. Some of those unsavory characters had tracked them down and were headed to the hotel. Halkov had gotten tipped off and realized he had to move them to another hotel.

"We went down the service elevator and out the kitchen door," Hill recounted. "We got in a taxi and drove around, across the Bosphorus Bridge to the Asian side, into a park where we parked for a while to see if we were being followed." Halkov then took them to a different hotel where they spent a fitful few hours before heading straight to the airport the next morning. Reporting back to

McGovern, Hill and Krull told him that the only option was to quit the country. The cost to try to fix the mess or start over was too high. The Turkish office was closed and the company shuttered, much to McGovern's dismay.

Yet, despite these hair-raising misadventures, the vast IDG empire remained a mostly stable, tranquil landscape. Hill always believed that decentralization was a "great system" and the benefits always outweighed the downside. The incidents in Russia and Turkey were the "two worst" examples of what can happen when you "allow extraordinary independence and minimal oversight to your business units around the world," Hill said. "But for every disaster, there were several dozen real successes. It was a cost of how Pat McGovern chose to operate his company, and the approach was hugely successful for a long time."

McGovern never wavered in that belief either. To that end, Hill set up a licensing agreement in Russia to allow IDG to continue doing business there. It was not as lucrative as a joint venture would have been, but it kept IDG in the market. Hill also returned to Turkey in 2002 and set up a licensing agreement with a local company to publish Turkish versions of *Computerworld* and *PCWorld*. Just to be safe, he recruited Halkov to accompany him yet again. "There were still unhappy people looking for us," Hill said.

HOW IT WORKS

Decentralization was not just about international expansion. The concept was firmly entrenched in IDG's domestic operations and played a major role in the company's growth and success. McGovern detested internal politics, and decentralization was an effective method for avoiding the inevitable squabbles among business units.

"*InfoWorld* had nothing to do with how *PCWorld* was doing," said Mac McCarthy, a 14-year IDG veteran who started in the 1980s as a news editor for *InfoWorld*. "You didn't make any deals with other publications, and one of the reasons was that when it came time for the quarterly results, Pat wanted you to be responsible for your publication. You couldn't say, 'Well, I would have done that if it hadn't been that *PCWorld* screwed up and didn't sell those extra ads.' It was the only company I've ever worked at where there were no corporate politics."

Pat Kenealy served in many roles in his 31-year career at IDG, including CEO of the company and head of several business units. He had a front-row seat to the leadership lessons taught by McGovern. His successful experience in the decentralized environment made a strong impression. According to Kenealy, IDG's decentralized structure was characterized by four commonalities:

1. **The rarity of visits from McGovern and other IDG headquarter executives.** "During four years as CEO of *PCWorld* Communications, Pat was in our building in San Francisco just three or four times a year," Kenealy said. "He'd attend three board meetings and then come out to hand out holiday cards and bonuses. He was *never* there otherwise. Walter Boyd, who was my boss for part of that time, never came!" Kenealy added that had his business unit been missing its budget projections, McGovern might have shown up more often, but that trust and faith he showed "was very empowering for the business unit manager." Clearly, based on the Russia and Turkey examples, there could be a significant downside to leaving a business unit alone for too long. Trusting country managers around the globe worked far more than it failed, but it did not come without risk.

2. **The budget process.** McGovern believed in giving business unit managers a wide berth, but he was not completely hands-off the corporate mission. Each year, he sent out short, general notes to all the business units, laying out his analysis for IT industry growth rates for the year to come. Business unit leaders would submit their budgets for approval and negotiate them at their board meetings, at

which McGovern was usually present. They rarely heard from headquarters after that unless they fell behind the budget projections for more than one quarter in a row. If that happened, the manager got a warning. Missing the budget for three quarters in a row usually cost that manager the job.

"There was never any remediation of business unit heads by Pat or his staff," Kenealy said. "They backed you or sacked you under the 'three quarters and out' rule." Decentralization couldn't work if there was no accountability, and McGovern, with his photographic memory, knew the budgets, the projections, and the results down to the penny. "If you made your numbers, you were the duke in your duchy or cardinal in your diocese," Kenealy said.

3. **Worldwide face-to-face meetings.** The secret sauce for successful decentralization is communication and transparency. IDG's Worldwide Managers Meetings brought all the business unit heads together once a year, usually in some exotic locale such as Hawaii, Alaska, Brazil, or China, to share market feedback, best practices, and perhaps most important, gossip. Strong and important relationships were formed that allowed country managers to share best practices with their colleagues, and the meetings made hierarchical management less imperative. There were similar worldwide meetings for publishers and for circulation directors, production managers, finance directors, and webmasters. McGovern paid for the meetings and attended parts of them, but he left early so that the participants could speak freely to each other. He also used the meetings to identify up-and-coming talent. He had a knack for spotting those who commanded the respect of their peers.

4. **Business unit managers get top billing over centralized services.** IDG had just a few centralized services

such as finance, key account sales, and competitive analysis. McGovern would often get pushback on this tenet of decentralization. As the company expanded around the globe, some clamored for centralized printing services and human resources, among other typical corporate functions, to take advantage of the scale and the cost savings. But the few centralized services at IDG were usually charged back explicitly to the business units and answered to "boards" made up of the business unit managers who paid the biggest bills. Clearly, this was not the cheapest way to run a media company, but it allowed IDG's publications to remain agile and aggressive compared to companies with centralized teams in finance, production, circulation, advertising, and the like. It also eliminated the creation of powerful central functions whose directors often fought with publishers about costs and drove many of them to other companies.

At heart, McGovern was an entrepreneur, and he loved other entrepreneurs who thought as he did. Sometimes, when a new executive joined IDG from outside, the cultures initially clashed. Robert Metcalfe, a fellow MIT graduate, who coinvented Ethernet and founded 3Com, a successful maker of computer networking equipment, joined IDG in 1990 as publisher and columnist for *InfoWorld*. He later became IDG's chief technology officer, and he didn't like what he saw.

"It disturbed me that each one of our magazines had its own printing contract," Metcalfe recounted. "That's a big deal; printing is a big cost. So I proposed that we have a corporate buying contract for printing and merge our printing requests. I just couldn't get the publishers to agree with this." Metcalfe turned to McGovern and made his pitch.

"The publishers don't want to take advantage of these incredible savings we would get if we just bought printing together," he told McGovern. And McGovern quickly replied, "Well, I prefer to pay the extra money for printing just to preserve the independence and entrepreneurial nature of the publisher's job at IDG."

Not surprisingly, in a half-century of overseeing this global organization, McGovern had to occasionally acquiesce to certain business realities, even if they flew in the face of his personal philosophy.

In 1989, for example, McGovern hired Kelly Conlin, a young Harvard MBA whom he eventually promoted to CEO of IDG. Conlin had the unpleasant task of suggesting a deviation in the decentralization playbook. Early in his IDG tenure, Conlin, as director of business development, started to get serious pushback from advertising clients such as IBM and Microsoft, who demanded a global relationship with all of IDG's publications that was consistent with their other strategic partnerships. IBM didn't want to have to make advertising arrangements with every individual publication around the world. That was simply too cumbersome and impractical. In fact, when Louis V. Gerstner Jr. was brought in as CEO to turn around IBM's sagging fortunes in 1993, one of his first edicts was to fire all of IBM's hundreds of advertising agency partners and bring in just one: Ogilvy & Mather.[3] He wanted coherence in IBM's corporate marketing and advertising. And Ogilvy & Mather turned around and told IDG, "We don't want to deal with 200 publications. We want to deal with one representative who can help us market our products globally across the IDG product portfolio."

To that end, Conlin set up the IDG Marketing Services division. It would mark the first time the company had a sales force designed to serve the largest customers in an integrated fashion. Needless to say, it was a controversial move and put Conlin on the hot seat. "Business units ran their own territory and they openly competed and the IDG portfolio was the better for it," Conlin said. "That's a very good business model for operating a company, but it is very customer *unfriendly*, when it comes to large clients like IBM or Microsoft."

Stuck in the middle of this quandary, Conlin tried to figure out his options. He had to find approaches that wouldn't derail the decentralized philosophy but would accommodate customers who demanded a single global account sales team.

"How do you do that in a way that doesn't take away the prerogative of the individual business unit, but instead is compatible and complementary with it?" he asked. He believed his new division could serve both masters.

The group was effective, but it produced decades of internal debate about its impact on staying close to the customer, which is one of IDG's 10 corporate values. McGovern was not a fan of the new group, despite the fact that it had a lot of success. "He realized the necessity of it," Conlin said, "but it went against his essential grain, and he would say it was rubbing things the wrong way." Conlin worked hard to overcome the internal politics arrayed to fight it. "It's not what we wanted to do, but the customers demanded it, and ultimately, it has been right over the long term as a way to create the best leverage for IDG properties for the benefit of our customers."

GETTING BUY-IN

IDG's evolution as a global giant had its glitches, but McGovern instinctively embraced decentralization, and even though he bent on this occasion, he never broke with the decentralized approach. He had given much thought to his management philosophy over the years, and in a 2000 *Computerworld* interview, he highlighted the results that demonstrated decentralization's effectiveness. He spoke about the kinds of bonus plans and employee stock ownership programs that made IDG a favored workplace.

"I always feel that people should have a stake in the economic success that they are contributing to," McGovern said. "In our decentralized style, where each business is a focused enterprise, and there are very strong bonus systems on individual achievement, the thing you want to promote is a motivation for sharing. Each business is doing a lot of R&D, trying lots of new things, learning a lot of new things. If they had no interest other than using those techniques themselves, then the success of our total system would lack the empowerment of that knowledge sharing."

To promote such sharing, McGovern initiated worldwide participation in IDG's employee stock ownership plan (ESOP), so that everyone would have skin in the game. "So when they get some request for help from France, or from Brazil, or Russia, and they give that help, and they help the success of that company, it boosts the value of IDG overall," he said. "So we are all benefitting."

Instead of triggering rivalries—and there was no lack of intra-IDG competition—the best business practices from every product line and every geography were redistributed around the world. During the company's heyday, the opportunity for young, emerging leaders to learn in what amounted to a global university, to improve their skills and hone their expertise, became a magnet for attracting new talent and a cornerstone for retaining existing managers.

For McGovern, one of the key barometers of decentralization's effectiveness was his painstaking dedication to measuring everything. In some cases, getting accurate, timely numbers was challenging. But McGovern always accepted occasional failures if the overall engine was humming smoothly. Being a math savant and a true believer that the numbers don't lie, he initiated detailed quarterly readership surveys and required country managers to do the same.

"We get the results and it is our way of monitoring how well they are performing in their own marketplace," McGovern said. "It would be impossible for us to go over and tell our German publishers how they should report to the German audience, or the Chinese, or Japanese or Indian. This way we get a very relevant and timely measure by insisting upon the feedback from these independent research studies."

What emerged over time was that the best jobs at IDG were out on the front lines. Talking to IDG executives, some no longer with the company, one theme developed: It might be nice to have a fancy title, but a job at IDG headquarters was not the desired position.

The action was out in the marketplace; the best experiences were had and most challenging work was done out in the business units. McGovern was well aware of this phenomenon. When IDG was at its zenith, between 1996 and 2000, with 13,000 employees around the world, the headquarters staff was just 19 people.

He didn't want people in roles that did little but get in other people's way. "In fact, any time there is a request for another business analyst or business development person to join IDG, I immediately put the request into my paper shredder," McGovern said. "Because what those people do is collect a huge amount of data and take up people's time. It is extremely expensive, and it doesn't really accomplish very much."

Sharing best practices among the business unit leaders was a key driver in growth and maintaining competitive leadership. Along with the ceaseless surveys of customers and employees and advertisers, the sharing of results and then having these leaders gather to offer the secrets behind the results was paramount for McGovern. "The biggest room in the world is the room to improve," he said.

Autonomy, he believed, triggered motivation. But it could also offer a convenient opportunity to undersell target projections. McGovern learned in the early days of IDG's global growth that when business unit managers came to Boston to discuss and explain their business plan for the next three years, these young leaders always hedged their bets and identified obstacles rather than paths to success. The head of IDG Italy, for example, would mention his difficulties with competitors, the economic problems plaguing the local market, and a long list of challenges. "We can only expect 2 percent revenue growth and 3 percent profit growth, and this is the best we can do," the Italian would declare.

It was difficult for McGovern to argue with this. He had designated these managers as experts in their local markets, so how could he challenge their assessments? So he decided to change the format and let psychology play a role. "We said, 'Don't present to us. Present to the heads of the other companies.'" McGovern explained. "There is a natural sibling rivalry within the company. All of a sudden we noticed the leader would say, 'We are a very efficient company. We have great people. I'm a wonderful leader. We're going to grow 25 percent in revenue and 30 percent profit growth. I'm going to be the best in our category.' We don't have to push them for performance. They are now doing it on pride."

For the better part of five decades, McGovern's blueprint paid significant dividends. Decentralization, for McGovern, was the fuel that kept the IDG engine humming. At one point, the legend goes, autonomy was so great that headquarters staff didn't know that an overseas operation had started a new publication until they received a copy of the first issue in the mail.

But as the twenty-first century moved into its second decade, market forces began to shift dramatically, and the realities of being in the media business became stark and sometimes ominous. Print began to give way to digital, and the Internet completely shifted the way information was shared around the world. This put intense pressure on a business model that strained under the weight. Until he died in 2014, the challenges only made McGovern more determined to stay his decentralized course. "He was incredibly consistent," Arnot said, "and in being consistent, he always owned a position of strength. People want to believe that they are part of something that's real, that's strong and has the resources, the intent, and the will. That is a leadership skill." In troubled geographies, or through difficult economic downturns, "Pat would still take a consistent approach—charismatic, strong—and he would say, 'Just remember, you are part of IDG. This is IDG.'"

TAKEAWAYS

➤ Find a fertile market and identify a need there that you can fulfill.

➤ Hire passionate local business leaders and put your trust in them.

➤ Listen to the market and be guided by your customers. Human nature is the same everywhere. Empower people and show empathy for their struggles, and this will engender great loyalty.

➤ Worldwide face-to-face meetings for country managers and business unit leaders provide communication and transparency, both essential to successful decentralization.

5

LESSON FOUR
Identify the Warriors

*It doesn't make sense to hire smart people
and then tell them what to do; we hire
smart people so they tell us what to do.*
—STEVE JOBS

In 1992, York von Heimburg was a brash 35-year-old executive at Markt & Technik, then the largest German IT publisher, when he was recruited by Walter Boyd to join IDG. It took Boyd four meetings over several months to convince the tall, dynamic German to come on board.

"When I hired him, I told Pat that I had just made the biggest find of my career, or I was making a very big mistake," Boyd recalled. "York was bigger than life and had an answer for everything. You wanted to believe everything he said but he was so self-assured that it was almost off-putting."

Von Heimburg's first assignment was to revitalize IDG's flagging *PC Welt*, Germany's version of *PCWorld*, which was slogging along with 30,000 readers and an eighth-place ranking among

German IT magazines. *Computerwoche*, the German version of *Computerworld*, had a dominant market position among B2B publications, but in the consumer space, IDG was nearly irrelevant. Boyd told von Heimburg, "Either you fix it or we stop the whole B2C business." It was a nearly hopeless situation, but von Heimburg, eager to make a strong first impression, took an aggressive stance.

At IDG's quarterly European managers meeting, von Heimburg was prepared to shake things up. He had told his wife, "This could be my first and last European managers meeting." His English was spotty, his manner brusque, and he was the new guy on the block. "There were rumors that there's a crazy Bavarian guy here, so that became my brand," he said. In the crowded conference room, amid his European peers, sat Pat McGovern.

The crazy Bavarian did his presentation, stating clearly that he needed to decrease the cover price, double the print rate, and completely change the content. Most important, he needed to invest in staff to heighten the quality and initiate a major marketing campaign. His intention was to relaunch the brand in September of that year, and he believed he could juice up sales if he could do it his way. Just four months into his tenure, he put together a $4 million budget proposal, the largest ever suggested to McGovern in his European ventures. It was a sum that no one had ever tried to pry out of the fiscally cautious McGovern, especially on a project that had already devoured several million dollars.

McGovern calmly responded, "York, that was a great presentation, but we at IDG have a different strategy. We do the best quality for the best price, which means high cover price. We don't double the print circulation. All this costs too much."

Brash and somewhat desperate, von Heimburg did the unthinkable and replied, "Pat, I know I'm young, but what doesn't work is shit quality for the highest price. That will never work."

People in the room gasped at von Heimburg's impertinence. He was calling out the chairman in front of a roomful of IDG veterans.

McGovern just smiled. Rather than show von Heimburg the exit, McGovern appreciated the maverick in him, and when they spoke later, McGovern gave him a green light for his plans. From the start, McGovern believed in hiring people who knew the needs of the local market and letting them follow their instincts. His policy of hiring good people and getting out of the way would be put to the test here. He let the remark pass and observed as von Heimburg oversaw a bold makeover of both the magazine and the marketing efforts. He realized this was an expensive bet, but he sensed something in von Heimburg that made him comfortable taking the risk.

Von Heimburg spent lavishly, including on television advertising, and he aggressively went after the newsstand market, which, in a country with 110,000 newsstands, is a dominant sales channel. With just a few months to revamp the publication, von Heimburg dropped the cover price from eight German marks to five, ordered a 200,000 copy print run for the first issue, and sold 100,000 copies right away, the rest over time. His hard-hitting marketing efforts paid dividends immediately and over the long haul. It was an impressive beginning. And then things really took off. Newsstand sales and subscriptions soared, and by 1995, circulation peaked at 500,000, making *PC Welt* the number one computer publication in Germany.

"I dominated the market because I was very aggressive," said von Heimburg, now president of International IDG Communications. "This was when Pat discovered I was an entrepreneur, and he gave me full responsibility and full trust to act. With that backing, you can really develop yourself into a great manager and leader."

For Boyd, von Heimburg's success validated his confidence, but like many a hire in a fully decentralized organization, the journey can be breathtaking and stress-inducing.

"He was on board for just four months, and he presented this budget and asked for an investment of $4 million," said an incredulous Boyd. "But York did it. He went off-script and resurrected *PCWorld* Germany."

THE RIGHT PERSON

"Effective leaders allow great people to do the work they were born to do," said Warren Bennis, the renowned leadership guru and author.[1]

Like the best leaders, McGovern had an innate ability to identify talent and recruit that talent to the company. He also made it part of the foundation of his leadership style to allow people to be great at the work he hired them to do. Because he thoroughly trusted his top lieutenants like Walter Boyd, he willingly accepted their recommendations, especially as IDG began to experience significant global growth. With his nearly religious conviction about building a decentralized organization, McGovern knew that this was, at the end of the day, a business completely reliant on finding and hiring the best and the brightest and stepping out of the way. IDG had grown so big that he couldn't do all this himself anyway. He believed deeply that intrinsic intelligence and hard work won over experience and academic credentials.

"Most people are only working at 15 percent of their capacity," he said. "If you give them a challenge, their skills and capabilities most definitely will flower. People will be happier and business performance will increase. Best of all, a lot of sour-faced middle managers will disappear."

To that end, McGovern hired his young leaders and continued his policy of limiting the size of the units to under 200 people, even as the business units continued to grow in revenue. He heard the "bigger-is-always-better" voices that called for ever-increasing growth and consolidation of business units to create scale and reduce expenses. But he believed they were wrong.

According to Jeffrey Rayport, the lesson was potent and distinct. "He identified the warriors and he'd empower them, back them, or arm them," Rayport said. "He would go into these untouched markets, at least untouched by IDG, and somehow he would sift through what in his mind was a short list of entrepreneurial talent. Would this talent cross over to tech and to media and to research? If it did, he would give them license to run something, along with capital and an almost unfettered authority."

Rayport, who had countless breakfast meetings with McGovern over the years, marveled at his insight about the importance of finding the right person at the right time. It was, McGovern believed, all about the selection process at the front end; identifying the entrepreneur or the talent that you could bet on to carry your brand, to deploy your capital, and to grow the franchise.

"That was the secret ingredient that made IDG go," Rayport said. "If you had a bunch of yes-men or company guys or suits, the system would have ground to a halt. Pat could identify gifted entrepreneurs and give them the wherewithal they needed to go be ten times as successful on Day One because he gave them capital, a brand, access to editorial content, and a mission."

McGovern understood the reality that most professionals, regardless of their talent level, lived in a risk-averse world where the safe bet was to join a big corporation, work your way up the ladder, and build a career. At the other extreme, there were the few hardy pioneers like himself or Bill Gates or Michael Dell who started businesses in their dorm rooms and took the ultimate risk of betting on themselves.

And somewhere in the middle, the sweet spot that McGovern mined for talent, were those with an appetite for entrepreneurial risk but who still wanted the comfort of operating from within the supportive arms of an existing organization. These intrapreneurs live and die by their own efforts, but they do so with an existing brand name, somebody else's intellectual property, a corporate back office, and a safety net. These were McGovern's leaders-in-training, and he was a mentor to a legion of them. They were ambitious, talented, and happy to take ownership of McGovern's vision. Many would go on to become corporate leaders in other settings. Michael Perlis, who ran IDG Peterborough, succeeded Hugh Hefner as publisher of *Playboy* magazine, and later became CEO of Forbes Media. Eric Hippeau left *InfoWorld* to become president and CEO of rival Ziff Davis, and later CEO of the Huffington

Post. John Griffin, president and publisher of *PCWorld*, went on to become president of Rodale's magazine division, COO at Hearst magazines, and later, president of the publishing division of the National Geographic Society.

In return for inventiveness and output, McGovern tolerated individual idiosyncrasies. He understood that in industries such as media, fashion, entertainment, and technology, leaders must learn to put up with eccentricity in exchange for creativity.

He made occasional mistakes, and he was a reluctant but determined enforcer. Though he personally avoided confrontations, he was the wrong executive to cross, and he could be relentless in righting what he perceived as egregious wrongs. Managers who didn't make their agreed-upon numbers did not last very long.

McGovern made bets on candidates who fell decidedly outside the boundaries of conventional wisdom, but his success rate far outweighed the failures. His hires could be young, quirky, compelling, and nonconformist. Well before it was politically correct, he hired gay executives like Boyd, simply because they were exceptional and shared his core passion and vision for the company. In fact, in the early 1990s, IDG became the second company in Massachusetts to offer spousal benefits to gay couples, along with unmarried heterosexual couples, a bold and controversial stance at the time that McGovern fully supported. He hired women in senior roles in various geographies, and he brought in a large cadre of people who were ridiculously young for the roles they were taking on. Some had only high school diplomas, but this never mattered to McGovern. He would help pay college tuition and promote based on performance and integrity rather than credentials. "He emboldened you to do things you otherwise wouldn't have done," said Bill Laberis, a former editor at *Computerworld*.

"I think he was playing with a very sophisticated model of how you unleash human potential and how you inspire people," Rayport added. "But also, how you structure opportunity for people so that you bring out the most entrepreneurial forms of their talent and behaviors."

THE WARRIORS

One of IDG's most ardent warriors was Hugo Shong, who, as we've seen, became IDG's leader in China. When McGovern decided to hire Shong, he asked what kind of compensation package Shong would require. Shong said he was less concerned about his compensation than about having direct access to McGovern, so he insisted on reporting directly to the chairman. "I felt that if I could communicate my excitement and promising proposals directly to him, he was the kind of person who would understand and take action quickly," Shong said.

McGovern accepted the terms, made Shong IDG's associate for Asia business development, and gave him a 20 percent salary bump from what he was earning at Cahners. Soon after, despite his lack of venture capital experience, Shong was chosen to head up IDG's new venture fund in China. It was a *Casablanca* moment, the beginning of a beautiful friendship. Many years later, Shong asked McGovern why, despite his inexperience, he had chosen him to manage the venture firm. With a wink, McGovern said, "Because you were the guy who was willing to bet your youth on China's future."

On the other side of the world in San Francisco, Pat Kenealy, an IDG veteran and one of three managing directors of IDG Ventures (now Ridge Ventures), the company's US venture capital fund, has embraced much of McGovern's leadership philosophy.

Kenealy, who served a stint as CEO of IDG, was as close to McGovern over his IDG career as anyone inside the company. He always had the sense that McGovern "was a computer guy who ended up in publishing," as opposed to a media mogul à la Rupert Murdoch or William Randolph Hearst. "He ended up running a media company because he thought that's what the IT revolution needed at the time, and he was right," Kenealy said.

Some of these warriors were women. Mary Dolaher, who served as McGovern's executive assistant and director of communications for 13 years, starting in 1981, was an example of McGovern's ability to identify and nurture talent, usually by throwing someone into the deep end of the pool and suggesting they swim. Working for McGovern was a master class in taking initiative. With no experience, Dolaher learned to plan massive IDG events such as the international managers meetings, the annual holiday party, and countless McGovern-inspired dinners around the world.

During her tenure, IDG built a thriving exhibition business to accompany its technology media empire. McGovern was an enthusiastic proponent of trade shows and sought opportunities in various sectors, including gaming. When IDG funded a start-up gaming magazine, *Infotainment World*, McGovern asked Dolaher to act as liaison to the new publication. Introduced to the gaming world, Dolaher began to take an active role in IDG's new video game industry shows, such as the newly launched Electronic Entertainment Expo (E3), which debuted in 1995.

When IDG turned to Mitch Hall Associates (MHA), a trade show operator, to run E3, Dolaher left IDG, joined MHA, and ran the show for the next 10 years. By then, Dolaher, married and starting a family, could no longer justify the extensive travel her job with McGovern required. This felt like a perfect opportunity. "I had good training," Dolaher said. "I had been doing events for Pat all around the globe anyway. Pat threw me into the flames all the time. He always made me feel confident that I could handle any obstacle. It was a great way to learn."

In 2006, Dolaher returned to IDG, made a bid for E3, and won the business. The show became part of IDG's World Expo. At a Saturday morning meeting over coffee, McGovern asked Dolaher to take charge of the World Expo business unit. "Pat taught me to surround myself with 'people you feel are smarter than you.' So I did just that, and it has made me more successful," she said. "He gave me all the tools I needed." Dolaher went on to become founder and CEO of IRL Events, an entertainment and technology show producer.

McGovern also favored bringing in young recruits who not only displayed an intuitive sense for the business but were also ready to be mentored and transformed into the warriors he needed.

Fresh out of Yale in 1980, Steve Woit attended a Radcliffe Publishing Course in Cambridge during the summer. A party sponsored by the *New Yorker* drew Woit to New York, and having just graduated, Woit thought it would be a great opportunity to find a job. At the party, he noticed Pat McGovern, standing off on his own, clearly apart from the swanky New York publishing scene swirling around him. Woit wandered over, introduced himself, and asked "What do you do?"

McGovern, in his genial manner, explained the computer publishing business, which was in full growth mode, and Woit expressed interest. McGovern handed him a business card and invited Woit to visit the Newton office. When Woit called about a week later, he was told McGovern was in China on business, which struck Woit as highly unusual, given how few Americans were doing business there at the time. He left messages and called back again. Finally, McGovern called him with an invitation to visit IDG and hear about some ideas he was formulating.

He told Woit to come up at 8 a.m. that Saturday. Woit, who lived in Connecticut, managed to get in his car at 6 in the morning, arrived on time, and found McGovern in the office by himself. Expecting an hour or two of McGovern's time, Woit spent the entire day talking to this impressive and unusual businessman. Early on, McGovern suggested Woit take his standard employment test, which Woit aced, and then he explained the vision he had for IDG.

"I felt he was the smartest person I had ever met," Woit said, which was meaningful after four years at Yale. "He not only had a tremendous amount of information about the industry and where it was going, but he also had this global view. He believed this industry would be global, and having grown up for some of my childhood in Paris, I was fascinated. I wanted to get involved in something global."

McGovern asked a lot of questions that were not usual in a job interview. "What do you like to do and what don't you like to do?" he asked, explaining that people tend to be good at things they like to do. "That's a very revealing question," Woit said.

He then asked Woit to sketch out a plan for starting a hypothetical bakery magazine. At just 22, Woit was amazed at the depth and direction of the interview. This guy was sharper by a wide margin than others with whom he had interviewed. Having just finished the publishing course at Radcliffe, he was ready with answers. Coincidentally, he had worked in a bakery all through high school, so he had a firsthand understanding of that unique environment.

Impressed by Woit's obvious talents, McGovern pulled out a job description for a position as executive assistant to the chairman for business analysis and development and made Woit an offer on the spot. The salary, which Woit etched into memory, was $14,400. Though he was ready to leap at the offer, Woit had several other job interviews set up for the following week and asked for some time to consider the offer. McGovern reluctantly agreed—he liked to close these deals quickly—but he pressed Woit to give him an answer in a week. Despite a better offer from Dun & Bradstreet, Woit had no doubt about where he would cast his lot.

During many of his 17 years at IDG, Woit worked closely with McGovern, soaking up his boss's uncanny abilities to see opportunities where others missed them, to empower people to reach beyond their own self-imposed limitations, and to dive into difficult business situations without fear. Among his assignments was to pull together what was essentially an IT media publishing guidebook, an actual manual based on the creation of *Computerworld*, *PCWorld*, *Macworld*, and other successful publications, that could be handed to managers launching new publications.

"This was literally a physical manual in a binder that you could hand to somebody in any country, and it would explain how to do these kinds of publications," Woit recalled. "It required me to learn the entire business."

When he left to start his own venture firm in 1997, Woit took with him McGovern's deeply etched influence. The lessons were indelible.

"He never looked back," Woit said. "He was always focused on what do we do now. If we had a terrible problem, he only wanted to talk about what we would do about it, not what caused it. He didn't dwell on things that weren't successful; he just moved on. And because he traveled so extensively to so many different cultures, he was always rewiring his brain. The Chinese have a different way of looking at things than the Europeans and the people in South America. He was always bringing back the best sort of knowledge of everything going on around the world. He would just soak it up."

Like a large cast of IDG managers and executives, Woit created an impressive résumé while being promoted to various jobs within IDG. One of the characteristics of McGovern's search for his warriors was a strong belief in promoting from within. He advocated hiring young, talented, and impressionable people and developing them in the context of his 10 corporate values and his family-like work environment. "Pat said, 'Bring them in. Let's train them. Bring them up through the system,'" said Bob Carrigan, who joined IDG as a college intern and ended up as CEO of IDG Communications. "He was happy with people who were there for a long time. He saw that as a real achievement."

Getting people engaged and excited about the mission and the culture mattered heavily in a business that relied on motivated knowledge workers. "It was an incredible master class working with Pat," said Carrigan, who later became chairman and CEO of Dun & Bradstreet. "His touch and the way he challenged people, the way he enabled people to do their best work. He was 100 percent consistent."

TAKEAWAYS

▶▶ Hire great people and let them follow their instincts.

▶▶ Most people are not working at their full capacity. Challenge them and their skills and capabilities will flower.

▶▶ Find those with an appetite for entrepreneurial risk and mentor them to become the company's leaders.

▶▶ Choose candidates who are young, quirky, and outside the boundaries of conventional wisdom.

▶▶ Throw people into the deep end and get them to do what they never believed they could do.

6

LESSON FIVE
"Let's Try It!" Encourage the Entrepreneurs

Ever tried. Ever failed. No matter.
Try again. Fail again. Fail better.
—SAMUEL BECKETT

In 1990, John Kilcullen was an ambitious young marketing executive based in New York's vibrant publishing community. At 31, Kilcullen was thinking about his future when he received a phone call from Jonathan Sacks at IDG. Sacks had recently been named CEO of a new division called IDG Books, and he was looking for a dynamic vice president of sales and marketing. Kilcullen's name had crossed his desk because he had worked for a large computer book publishing company in Indianapolis and seemed to be the kind of proactive self-starter Sacks was seeking. Sacks arranged to meet Kilcullen at the Helmsley Hotel in New York City, a lunch that would dramatically alter Kilcullen's career. At the time, Kilcullen had designs on starting his own publishing company. Sacks said, "Why don't you start your company on our nickel?" That question struck a chord, and Kilcullen agreed to sign on and move from New York to California to help launch the new book division.

Just three weeks later, Sacks, the former editor and publisher of IDG's *InfoWorld*, was pulled back to that publication when the new publisher, enmeshed in internal turmoil, abruptly left. *InfoWorld* was a key tabloid for the company as IDG aimed to spread its dominance in the hypercompetitive personal computer space. Sacks told a stunned Kilcullen of his impending departure and promoted him, on the spot, to publisher of IDG Books Worldwide. Having signed up to run sales and marketing, Kilcullen was now in charge. He felt both exhilarated and very alone. He had dreams of running the show but not this quickly.

"Within three weeks," Kilcullen recalled, "I was running a P&L for a book publishing company, having never run a P&L or published a book before. What the heck did I just get myself into?"

Fortunately for Kilcullen, he was in the right company to become an intrapreneur. Among the most essential of IDG's 10 corporate values was the one closest to Pat McGovern's heart: "Let's try it." Many a young IDG manager was thrown into the deep end of some publishing venture to either sink or swim, so Kilcullen was not alone. He also shared many of McGovern's business values, especially the notion that staying close to the customer was the key to success.

Few CEOs encouraged entrepreneurial behavior more than McGovern. He believed in developing talent, usually from within, and immersing these young Turks in the IDG system and corporate values. A simple note to McGovern with an innovative idea and a decent business plan would usually receive a clear message to go for it and initial funding.

In so doing, he empowered several generations of young, untested but talented employees to perform well beyond their own expectations. This environment spawned a reputation that IDG was among the best places to work in the industry, and people clamored for jobs. In China, a job at *China Computerworld* was so coveted that its employees were considered among the elite in the job market.

But while encouraging, "Let's try it" does not guarantee the sought-after outcome. IDG's roadside was littered with its share of failed start-ups. Forays into technology television, a rolling computer caravan conference effort, and a magazine focused on Digital Equipment Corporation were among the best-laid plans that came to naught. IDG Books looked like it might suffer the same fate.

For about a year, Kilcullen tried to jump-start the new publishing unit. The outcome was disappointing. The original model for IDG Books was to publish branded books based on the titles of IDG publications such as *InfoWorld*, *PCWorld*, *Macworld*, and *GamePro*. But the effort was producing tepid results. With IDG's original $1.5 million investment dwindling down to $200,000, Kilcullen decided to rethink the entire concept.

He recalled a dinner in New York City in 1987 with a couple of industry friends. Over dinner, one member of the group told a story of being in a software store—perhaps CompUSA—and he overheard a customer walk up to a clerk and say, "I need a book on MS DOS, something really low level for me, you know, like DOS for Dummies."

The imaginary title stuck in Kilcullen's mind over the years, and then in 1991, he had an aha moment. "Right when you are running out of cash is when ideas are born," he said, "and in this case, I had a feeling that this was an idea that could stick."

The concept was simple but profound: a series of technology books for the curious but uninformed user trying to make sense of the burgeoning world of personal technology. In the early nineties, well before the ubiquity of the Internet, years before the advent of Google and YouTube, people had countless questions about computers and few places to turn for the answers. Cumbersome user manuals were filled with jargon and indecipherable instructions and created more headaches than solutions. What Kilcullen foresaw was a series of cleverly written reference guides "for dummies" that would ease the agony at the intersection of neophytes and computers. The customer premise was clear and inviting: "You're smart, but you're being made to feel dumb. Let us help you in plain, simple English and not take ourselves too seriously."

Kilcullen circulated his idea internally at IDG to get feedback on the For Dummies book series, starting with *DOS for Dummies*. He vividly recalls the editor in chief of *PCWorld* responding, "That would be a really bad idea, to call our customers dummies. It would hurt the IDG brand and the IDG ethos." He suggested calling it *The PCWorld Guide to DOS*.

But the person he had to convince was McGovern. Not surprising, McGovern took a measured approach. Throughout his career, McGovern was savvy enough to know what he didn't know and to follow the lead of those he trusted who did know. He realized that Kilcullen was the only member of the new division who actually had experience in the technology and computer book sector. "He really allowed his champions in a decentralized world to pursue their points of view," Kilcullen said.

McGovern's sharp focus was on whether or not his people were staying close to the market, understanding customer needs, having data to underline their strong convictions about the right way to proceed. He was laser-focused on the top line, on profits, on expenditures. Though McGovern was not shy about pushing back on ideas, he felt Kilcullen was close enough to the customer to support his concept. The idea of using *dummies* in the book title clearly vexed him, but he didn't say a word.

"There was never a dissenting view," Kilcullen recalled, "but you could read the nonverbal cue that it wouldn't have been his first choice."

McGovern's encouragement and support of IDG entrepreneurs was already legendary. The wins had always far outweighed the losses. This might be a risk, but most of the best outcomes began as risks. He gave Kilcullen his approval, and the rest became publishing industry legend.

The For Dummies series launched just before the holidays in 1991 with *DOS for Dummies* by Dan Gookin. The first printing was a cautious 7,500 copies. Some of the major bookstore chains refused to carry it, claiming the title insulted their customers. But they quickly changed their minds when the book became an immediate hit. The volume included a series of clever cartoons by computer cartoonist Rich Tennant, which became a popular staple of future titles. Word of mouth spread quickly, tens of thousands of copies were sold, and IDG Books had a tiger by the tail. Multiple printings ensued, and Gookin, who was paid a paltry $6,000 advance, eventually made "an absolute trash load of money," as he described it in a *Slate* magazine interview. The book eventually sold more than 1 million copies.

DOS for Dummies, the beginning of a global brand.

Kilcullen, a marketing savant, focused on the book design, and the distinctive black-and-yellow volumes began to dot bookstore shelves. "I learned from my days on Madison Avenue, you have three points to advertising: (1) get their attention, (2) deliver a message, and (3) motivate them to action." In this way, Kilcullen turned a single bestseller into a burgeoning global brand, an outcome that delighted McGovern. Over the ensuing years, various theories emerged about who conceived the original Dummies title. More than a few people took credit, and Kilcullen has heard them all. "Success has many fathers," he said. Regardless, there is no doubt who shepherded the idea for more than a decade into its wildly successful existence.

The first 17 titles were all focused on technology: *Windows for Dummies, Mac for Dummies, Unix for Dummies,* and so on. The concept struck a major chord. *Windows for Dummies* alone sold more than 10 million copies. But Kilcullen wasn't satisfied. He saw a broader opportunity in the consumer marketplace. There were literally limitless subjects, from finance to football, from music to medicine, that begged for a reference book that spoke to the information-seeking neophyte. He settled on his first nontechnology title—*Personal Finance for Dummies*—and in so doing, he crossed an important IDG boundary. IDG's mission—to educate information technology professionals through information technology media—had been inviolable and successful. This was a leap into a consumer space that McGovern had long avoided.

Signing off on a quirky title was one thing, but moving beyond the IT market caused no small amount of discomfort for McGovern. Kilcullen sat down with the CEO and explained the logic, and his arguments were persuasive. McGovern "simmered" with the idea, and ultimately acknowledged that he couldn't argue with the financial results, the margins, the top line revenue, and the growing profits. Kilcullen argued that the books would still represent IDG's vision to spearhead global technology literacy, but that literacy could be extended in new directions and still fulfill the expectations of IDG's customers. Beyond that, Kilcullen had done a masterful job of creating branded content, as well as installing an efficient and successful process in conceiving, acquiring, and producing new titles on a timely and cost-effective basis.

Kilcullen recalled the conversations he had with the laser-focused McGovern. The For Dummies brand had surpassed all financial yardsticks. "We can't stop because of some predetermined sensibility that we will offend someone," Kilcullen argued.

McGovern acknowledged that the For Dummies brand transcended IDG's traditional market, and he backed off his objections. "He was not going to say, 'I forbid it'; that was not his way," Kilcullen said. Instead, McGovern quietly invoked corporate value #10 and said, "Let's try it."

Thus began an avalanche of new titles: *Golf for Dummies*, *Wine for Dummies*, and even *Sex for Dummies* by famed radio sex therapist Dr. Ruth Westheimer. That last one sent shivers through IDG's executive committee, which balked at going that far. Nonetheless, the title was published, became a massive success, and garnered a tidal wave of global publicity without costing IDG a penny.

The For Dummies brand was wildly successful, beyond anyone's imagination. No subject was considered too eclectic, and titles such as *Baby Massage for Dummies*, *Raising Goats for Dummies*, and *Dyslexia for Dummies* found their way to bookstore shelves. Kilcullen had created a game-changing international brand. It became impossible to visit a bookstore without encountering the familiar and suddenly ubiquitous black-and-yellow book covers.

The books spawned music CDs, board games, and toys. Offers came in to take it to the movies and television, and Kilcullen eventually hired International Creative Management, a Hollywood talent agency, to oversee the foray. For a brand to quickly become so much a part of popular culture was a huge win for IDG, taking it swiftly and powerfully into the consumer marketplace. By 1998, there were more than 350 For Dummies titles with 50 million copies in print, and the titles regularly dotted bestseller lists. Revenues would soar to nearly $250 million by 2000.

IDG Books was so successful, in fact, that McGovern was persuaded to forgo yet another long-held principle of his business bible. In 1998, the IDG Books unit filed an IPO as a test to see how IDG as a whole might fare in the public markets. McGovern,

The 5th Wave

By Rich Tennant

"Alright, steady everyone. Margo, go over to Tom's PC and press 'Escape'...very carefully."

"Clawface" by Rich Tennant. His cartoons became a staple of the Dummies books.

despite occasional suggestions to employees that he might one day take IDG public, believed with almost religious fervor in maintaining a private company. He never wanted the onerous burden that quarterly earnings reports and Wall Street investors would put on his ability to steer the company as he saw fit. But with the growing frenzy around dot-com IPO fever in the late 1990s, he acquiesced.

IDG brought in Morgan Stanley and Merrill Lynch to handle the public offering and IDG Books, renamed "Hungry Minds, Inc.," offered shares to the public. In this era, which Federal Reserve chairman Alan Greenspan described as "irrational exuberance," the assumption was that any high-tech offering would quickly have a market cap in the billions. The offering raised about $200 million, but Wall Street viewed the company as a publishing play rather than a hot technology offering, and the stock price stagnated.

As time went on and the stock underperformed expectations, the underwriters complained that the unit was not growing fast enough, so Kilcullen began making acquisitions. McGovern had always given business unit leaders tremendous leeway as long as the numbers met or exceeded expectations. But he also let it be known that IDG's success had been built by investing frugally and wisely. He eschewed spending heavily on infrastructure, for example, because owning capital-intensive real estate and plants was not good for the bottom line. Nonetheless, he didn't object when Kilcullen began making costly acquisitions such as the CliffsNotes study guides, Frommer's travel guides, Betty Crocker cookbooks, and the Webster's New World Dictionary, among others. He was focused on fast growth, but the acquisitions left the company with a heavy debt load. There was increasing competition from the "Idiot's Guides" published by Penguin Putnam. And then, as the dot-com meltdown struck in 2000, the book publishing industry got hit hard.

In fact, IDG Books was not the only IDG property struggling to cope with the suddenly volatile market. An expensive, complicated, and ultimately unsuccessful investment in the once vaunted but quickly defunct *Industry Standard*, an Internet business magazine, was a painful experience for McGovern during the dot-com meltdown in 2001. Burdensome leases and profligate spending during the dot-com bubble had left the *Industry Standard* nosediving toward bankruptcy.

For IDG Books, sales dropped precipitously. Suddenly, it could not meet its debt payments. Under pressure from creditors, the company was sold in September 2001, for $90 million in cash, to John Wiley & Sons. Wiley also assumed about $90 million more in debt.[1] Had it not been sold, IDG Books might have ridden the For Dummies brand much further to significant future profits. Today, more than a quarter century after it first appeared, the brand continues to have legs, with nearly 2,500 titles and more than 300 million copies in print around the world.[2] But lamenting the sale was not McGovern's style. In fact, the entire effort had proved to be a win-win for IDG, which reaped millions of dollars from the For Dummies phenomenon, and for Kilcullen, who emerged a wealthy man with an impressive set of credentials, having built a highly successful international brand from scratch.

As always, McGovern refused to focus on yesterday's setbacks. The IDG Books IPO served to confirm his doubts about public companies, but ultimately, the future was where success lay, and there were many more wins than losses built upon "Let's try it."

AHEAD OF THE CURVE

As often happened, McGovern was a good decade ahead of his peers and competitors when it came to fostering innovation within IDG. The concept of "intrapreneurship" gained wide popularity in the 1980s as innovation became the watchword for late twentieth-century corporate success. Leaders such as Steve Jobs, Richard Branson, and later Larry Page and Sergey Brin were vocal proponents of "Let's try it." The payoffs were world-changing. The list of breakthrough products and services spawned by internal innovation efforts is impressive. Among them:

- Apple's iPhone, iTunes, iPod, and iCloud

- Google's Gmail

- Sony's PlayStation

- 3M's Post-it Notes

- Virgin Air and Virgin Galactic

McGovern foresaw the power of such thinking from the earliest days of IDG. His decision in 1978 to get off a plane in Beijing without a visa to visit a country that had yet to establish diplomatic ties with the United States was a classic "Let's try it" moment that eventually spawned a highly lucrative result. His business sensibility mirrored his personality. He was driven, tireless, and highly competitive, but he had no craving for the spotlight or the lion's share of the credit. He made sure senior leaders within IDG were publicly feted and rewarded for out-of-the-box thinking that drove growth. Worldwide managers meetings were inspiring gatherings during which top performers were lauded by their peers and given cash rewards. By encouraging and supporting this kind of entrepreneurial spirit within IDG, the company reaped massive benefits.

For example, after 15 years working for IDC, most of that time as vice president of marketing, Joe Levy believed that the money and the fun were on the publishing side of the business. IDC, the company's research arm, had struggled unsuccessfully toward profitability for much of that time. But Levy had soldiered on until 1986 when IDC hired Carl Masi as its new CEO. Masi came from Wang Laboratories, at the time a noted minicomputer maker, and he had some big ideas about how to improve IDC's lagging fortunes. At an early 1987 executive committee meeting, Masi presented a grandiose plan to McGovern that involved spending a lot of money and making significant investments. Several IDC managers presented similarly optimistic plans, and then Levy, as VP of marketing, spoke last.

He had one foil for the overhead project: a picture of the sinking of the *Titanic*. "I looked at Pat, and I'm not a particularly brave person, but I said, 'Pat, we don't stand a chance in hell,'" Levy said. "Needless to say, that didn't ingratiate me with Carl Masi, who was my new boss."

Indeed, after the meeting, Masi took Levy into his office and told him he'd be gone in six months, so he ought to start looking for a new job. Levy did just that. But instead of looking outside the company, he thought about McGovern's edict: Let's try it. And he came up with an idea that had been percolating in his head.

IDC had been publishing countless reports about the heads of data processing as they were becoming more and more crucial to the business side of their firms. Despite their growing importance, these techies rarely received the respect and acknowledgment from corporate executives. They were considered integral parts of the back office but not savvy business leaders. Levy thought about all the C-level titles, from CEO to CFO, and thought, "Why not have a chief information officer, a *CIO*?" And beyond that, why not create a magazine for and about CIOs "and make them famous for their use of technology instead of just writing about the technology itself?" Levy thought.

He sent a note to McGovern with his idea, and not surprisingly, McGovern responded by saying "Give me a business plan." Levy knew little about business plans, but he put something together quickly and sent it along. His actual goal, he recalled, was simply to outlast Carl Masi, a fellow whom he assumed would flame out quickly in IDG's unique environment, and then Levy could return to his day job running marketing at IDC.

Levy figured he could spend at least several months researching the concept, mostly by visiting these CIOs and polling them to see if there was an audience for the prospective publication. He quickly realized he had tapped into something serious.

"I would be talking to people, and they would ask when the first issue was coming out," Levy recalled. "So I would make up a date. But as time went on, they'd ask me for a rate card."

Levy, in his marketing capacity at IDC, had coordinated magazine supplements based on IDC research for *Fortune* magazine. He helped the *Fortune* salespeople sell advertising and learned about *Fortune's* advertising rates. The supplements had been extremely profitable for *Fortune* and were moneymakers for IDC, so when asked about his new magazine, he quoted just below *Fortune's* rate card.

Nonetheless, he was quoting close to the highest cost per thousand readers (CPM) rate in the magazine world. At the time, he never envisioned an actual magazine being born. This whole effort was a stalling tactic. But as Levy played it out, he got a faint inkling that his stalling tactic was morphing quickly into an actual publication.

Levy came up with an initial circulation figure of 25,000, and as the fictional ad deadline for the first issue approached, he began to get panicky. "I figured this was a nice buildup of frequent flyer miles, but what I didn't realize was that to a lot of these advertisers, it sounded like a great idea," he said. "We started getting insertion orders for ads, and I finally had to tell Pat, 'We've got a big problem.' Pat said, 'What problem?' and I said, 'We have insertion orders for a magazine that doesn't exist.' And he said, 'It does now!'"

Thus *CIO* magazine was born, albeit without any editorial, sales, or production staff. Suddenly thrust into an editorial role, Levy fought off panic. He thought he might approach *Computerworld*, IDG's highly successful flagship publication, and make *CIO* a supplement to the weekly newspaper. But McGovern nixed the idea.

Years later, he confided to Levy that he was convinced that an association with *Computerworld* would have caused *CIO* to fail. *Computerworld*, McGovern reasoned, would have insisted on doing everything by the book, and that was exactly what Levy was avoiding. His plan and his advertising rates were audacious, and McGovern believed that audacity was what fueled *CIO*'s success.

CIO debuted in 1987 and was profitable from the start. Levy began with low overhead: just four employees, including himself and a coterie of freelancers. Once the magazine got traction, he initiated a series of executive conferences for CIOs in order for advertisers to mingle with top technology executives. Seemingly everything Levy did turned to gold. *CIO* found an instant and appreciative audience right out of the gate. Being on a *CIO* cover, which bore a slight resemblance to *TIME* magazine, became a badge of honor. Due to the magazine's cachet, exhibitors paid a steep price—up to $50,000—to attend the conference and were also required to pay $250,000 in advertising dollars for a 12-month period.

At its height under Levy, *CIO* became an $80 million business unit of IDG. McGovern was pleased. "As long as I made my numbers, I would never see him or hear from him," Levy said. "He'd send me ideas from time to time, but I ran it as if it was my own company."

INDIA TRIES IT

McGovern's ideology transcended corporate boundaries. He constantly encouraged young people he met to push themselves beyond their own expectations. His nephew, Gore Verbinski, an Oscar-winning Hollywood filmmaker who directed *Pirates of the Caribbean* and *Rango*, recalled his childhood when visits from Uncle Pat were "like a tornado blowing through."

When Verbinski was a 15-year-old neophyte guitarist with a garage band, McGovern came for a visit, heard the band rehearsing, and asked Gore if the band had a demo tape. Of course they didn't. They were 15-year-old kids just learning their instruments. But McGovern said, "You have to have a demo tape." It was Sunday, but he called around, found a recording studio, and booked two hours for his nephew's band. Though they were kids, they were ambitious and were writing their own songs. With the tape, the band was able to book parties and clubs to play their original tunes, and Verbinski learned a valuable life lesson about the power of the "Let's try it" attitude.

"If you wanted to run, he'd give you the shoes," Verbinski said. "But you had to run the race yourself. He eliminated the excuse that there are some circumstances that you can blame your failures on. He gave you that opportunity to prove your capabilities and to see clearly where you need improvement because you are doing it, rather than talking about it."

In similar fashion, albeit on a different scale, McGovern had a dramatic impact in India. There, McGovern encountered Sudhir Sethi, a pioneering venture capitalist based in Bangalore. IDG's entrance into the venture capital business, beginning in the United States in 1996, was proving to be the new financial bedrock for the company, and McGovern foresaw opportunity around the globe. Sethi was a catalyst in India's nascent venture capital industry, becoming an advisor to start-ups in 1998 and seeking out disruptive, high-growth technology firms with strong leadership teams.

By 2006, Sethi was ready to launch his own fund. In May, he received a call from an acquaintance saying that Pat McGovern wanted to meet him. The venture community in India was small, so fellow VCs were aware of Sethi's ambition. Sethi had never heard of McGovern or IDG, but when he Googled McGovern, he realized that he was meeting someone special.

McGovern, the opportunistic visionary, believed that venture capital would become a burgeoning sector in India. He trusted, from his past experiences in the United States, China, Vietnam, and South Korea, that venture would be good for the Indian people and the economy, and of course, a lucrative business opportunity for IDG. In his well-tested formula, McGovern knew he needed the right person to bring that vision into reality. He hoped Sethi was that person who would turn "Let's try it" into a success.

Sethi arranged a half-hour meeting with McGovern at the Oberoi Hotel in Bangalore at 9:30 in the morning. McGovern appeared with his wife, Lore, and the half-hour meeting turned into more than two and a half hours. "Sometimes one gets lucky," Sethi recalled. "We hit it off very well."

In his signature style, McGovern picked Sethi's brain with pointed questions about the Indian venture market, the local ecosystem, entrepreneurship in India, and the prospective markets that were attractive. Mostly, he wanted to know about Sethi.

They talked about Sethi's life, family, and ambitions. "We had immediate chemistry," Sethi said. "He was such a nice person, and he was very humble. I knew in the first half hour that this was someone I could look up to."

McGovern requested a written outline of Sethi's planned venture fund, and Sethi complied with a four-page document. A week later, McGovern called with some questions. Then Sethi started to hear from friends that McGovern had been making calls around the Indian network to learn more about him. McGovern sought out 9 or 10 of Sethi's compatriots and was clearly impressed by what he heard.

A month later, on June 21, Sethi got a call at home at 9 p.m. It was McGovern. He got right to the point.

"How much are you raising?" he asked Sethi about his new fund.

"$100 million," Sethi replied.

"How about raising $150 million," McGovern countered. "You should raise that much."

"I would if I could," Sethi said. "I need somebody to anchor my fund."

"IDG will anchor your fund," McGovern said without hesitation. In his classic "Let's try it" mode, he told Sethi he would provide the full $150 million.

Sethi was stunned. He thought somebody was playing a prank on him. He asked McGovern to hold, put down the phone, and turned to his wife to tell her what was happening. "You silly man," she admonished. "Why did you put down the phone?" When he regained his composure, Sethi picked up the phone and said, "Thank you, I will accept your offer."

With that, IDG Ventures India was founded on September 1, 2006, and Sethi became chairman and managing general partner. His cofounder and partner, T. C. Meenakshisundaram (or TCM), became managing director. McGovern came to visit, and Sethi offered to introduce his team. McGovern said he didn't need to meet the team members. He had full faith in Sethi. Sethi was once again astonished. Here was a global risk taker, a major success in information technology media but also a pioneer in venture capital in Asia. The idea that this man had put his full faith in him elevated Sethi's sense of responsibility to McGovern a hundredfold. And McGovern wasn't done.

Sethi and TCM knew they had to pay the team members' salaries until the fund got off the ground, and without the initial capital on hand, Sethi was prepared to sell his home. In August, he got a call from McGovern. "How are you going to pay your people?" McGovern asked. Sethi told him not to worry about it. "But you aren't getting any fees right now," McGovern replied. "I hope you aren't going to do something stupid, like sell your home." Sethi lied and assured him he had no intention of doing that. But before he had to face the payroll issue, McGovern, unprompted, sent a million dollars to capitalize the start-up fund.

"Pat placed his trust in me personally and in my team, and he helped us build one of the top three funds in the country," Sethi said. Among IDG Ventures India's 70 investments were Flipkart, India's version of Amazon and a leading e-commerce player, Myntra, an online fashion and sports retailer, Manthan, a global analytics product play, and Aujas, a global security firm.

McGovern counseled Sethi to seek out other limited partners for future funds, and he pledged to visit India as often as he visited China. Though he made more than a dozen trips to India, McGovern didn't have a chance to match his remarkable number of China visits, but he was in Bangalore often enough to do what he loved most: meet people, learn about the culture, and scope out new business opportunities.

Along the way, Sethi visited McGovern in Boston and California, and the pair talked for hours. McGovern shared his global outlook: how to identify markets, how to scale companies, how to find the best people and let them lead without corporate interference. He put Sethi's team in touch with IDG venture folks in China, Vietnam, South Korea, and the United States.

"He trusted people," Sethi said. "He gave me a platform, and his trust was no small thing. He went all the way, he was all in. He was a father figure to us, a guru."

McGovern was not altruistic about these investments. He pressed Sethi to exceed his own expectations. When Sethi told him he was aiming at a $200 million second fund, McGovern spoke to a business reporter in India and suggested IDG Ventures would raise $350 million. "I said, 'You should have talked to me first,'" Sethi said. "He said, 'You were not around.' That was Pat McGovern for you."

IDG Ventures India has been highly profitable. The firm emerged as one of the top venture firms in India, and IDG became a highly visible and respected brand name in that market.

"Pat showed faith in Sudhir and his team by truly being supportive, never intrusive," said Pat Kenealy, managing partner of IDG's US venture firm. "Pat could get testy if returns were slow to come, but he had patience for the ups and downs of India's economy, currency, and tech cycles."

As he did with most of his senior people, McGovern engaged in a warm personal relationship with Sethi and took every opportunity to spend time with him, his team, and his family. This helped to motivate Sethi when times were tough and to celebrate when times were good.

"IDG Ventures India is a classic example of Pat finding a good opportunity, identifying an able champion, and supporting, encouraging, and trusting that champion to build an organization appropriate to the locale and timing of the opportunity," Kenealy said. "Sound familiar?"

McGovern's leadership formula was built upon an unwavering sense of optimism that infused IDG and its outposts all over the world. This upbeat outlook served as a potent business tactic.

TAKEAWAYS

- ▶▶ Encouraging entrepreneurial behavior within an organization requires serious commitment, not just lip service.

- ▶▶ In so doing, an organization will get a reputation for being a desirable workplace and recruitment will improve.

- ▶▶ As long as people stay close to the market and the customer, a "Let's try it" approach will pay significant dividends.

- ▶▶ If your people want to run, give them the means and then step out of the way.

- ▶▶ There will be missteps and failures along the way, but "Let's try it" will result in far more wins than losses.

7

LESSON SIX
The Best Is Yet to Come:
Optimism Is Infectious—Use It

Optimism is an essential ingredient of innovation.
How else can the individual welcome change
over security, adventure over safe places?
—ROBERT NOYCE,
cofounder of Intel

Being at the helm of any enterprise for 50 years is a remarkable feat of endurance and persistence. The mere fact that the organization exists for that long is evidence of strong leadership and sound judgment. But it also means an inevitable list of bumps, stumbles, and even failures along the way. Business, after all, is governed by a series of sine waves that ebb and flow in cycles— periods of growth disrupted by occasional interludes of decline. Pat McGovern knew the push and pull of economic volatility and uncertainty. He entered the information technology media marketplace in its infancy and built a global organization that experienced tremendous growth but also sporadic periods of stagnation.

Risk takers know that a certain percentage of new ideas will struggle or fail. Being in the technology space meant riding an unpredictable roller coaster as trends shifted and evolved faster than many people could absorb. In five short decades we've moved from room-sized mainframe computers to pocket-sized supercomputers able to access all the information known to mankind. That remarkable journey was neither easy nor intuitive. Thousands in giant corporations and garage-based start-ups joined in, and most were lost along the way.

The landscape is littered with also-rans, never-weres, and might-have-beens. What was remarkable about McGovern was that he was not only unperturbed by these disruptions, he also remained an unfettered optimist no matter the economic circumstances. He was a leader who ended every important company gathering with his signature phrase: The best is yet to come!

Great leaders are adept at telling the organization's story in a way that makes it inspiring and infectious. McGovern's affability and genuine affection for his employees provided an entrée for IDG's workforce to enthusiastically enlist for the mission. He was Uncle Pat, a good guy but also a really smart guy. How could you not want to be part of his team? He had a similar effect on customers and advertisers, who may have been less enamored but still bought into the idea that IDG had something special going on that they wanted to be a part of.

"He had an incredibly positive attitude," said Bill Sell, a former IDG vice president who began working for the company at age 18. "The glass was always half full, even if there was only a tenth of water in the glass. He had that ability to find a way to encourage people even in the worst of situations."

"He had a remarkable ability to know what he wanted done. Even though you didn't want to do it, he made you do it and then sent you a Good News memo about the fantastic innovation you'd achieved," added Frank Cutitta, an IDG veteran who sold international advertising and often traveled overseas with McGovern. Today, Cutitta is a professor of communications at Northeastern

University. "I still teach this to my students," Cutitta said. "You did these things you might not have wanted to do, but he got you to do it and then congratulated you. It was fascinating how that worked in your mind."

McGovern realized a simple but profound truth: optimism is contagious. In the business environment, a positive, optimistic outlook spawns followers who want to be part of an effort, who feel good about their organization, and who tend to seek that intersection of a positive vision mixed with sometimes harsh business realities.

"He was a master at not pulling the plug, not giving up on something too soon," Sell said. "In a typical company, you get one quarter of bad results, and by the second quarter, it is game over. With Pat, he would see through business downturns, and as long as there was forward progress and the idea made sense, he would let it continue." Though his sometimes stubborn refusal to pull the plug on a stagnant enterprise at times pulled down IDG's results, more often, McGovern's steadfastness paid dividends. As the company grew larger, he invoked his "three bad quarters and out" rule, which while not set in stone, made it tougher on company managers to ride out long dry stretches.

David Hill, the longtime IDG executive who was responsible for licensing and worldwide subsidiaries, recalled a trip to London in 1988 to meet a Nigerian publisher named Samuel Ochapa from Lagos. Ochapa had contacted Hill in hopes of obtaining a license to launch *PCWorld* West Africa in Lagos to serve Nigeria and surrounding countries. "We met in London to go over his business plans and his thoughts on the technology industry in Africa," Hill said.

When he returned to Boston, Hill sat down with McGovern and recounted his meeting with Ochapa and what he had in mind. Hill hedged his bets. He said he liked the deal, but he didn't want anyone asking him a few years down the road why IDG had been wasting its time in a place like Nigeria. "I explained that if we did this license, we were not likely to see enough royalties in the next ten years to pay for the trip I had just made to London," Hill said. "Did he still want me to do the deal? Without hesitation, Pat said, 'Absolutely do it. Someday there will be a vibrant tech industry in Africa, and we need to be there and grow up with it,'" Hill recalled. In the years to come, IDG built successful operations in Nigeria, Kenya, and South Africa.

"He was a real cultural visionary," said Bob Carrigan, a former veteran IDG executive. "People talk about him as a publishing or technology visionary. To me, he was an amazing cultural visionary in that he understood how to activate and energize the employee base around a pretty big vision."

LIFE IS GOOD

Life Is Good is a $100 million, Boston-based retail clothing and giftware giant whose brand is based solely on an effort to spread the power of optimism. Bert Jacobs, the company's cofounder, writes a column for *Inc.* magazine about optimism in leaders. "Pessimistic leaders focus on obstacles," he wrote. "They make lists of reasons ideas won't work.... Pessimism causes close-mindedness.... Optimistic leaders focus on opportunities. Optimism is magnetic.... Optimists invent solutions that become genuine points of difference in the market. And points of difference in the market build healthy businesses."[1]

Eternal optimism, the laser focus on the positive, was McGovern's de facto management creed. He believed in his vision, acknowledged that some efforts could turn bad, but never spent significant time dwelling on the failures. This didn't come without repercussions. He was notoriously averse to confrontation and delegated bad news to be delivered by Walter Boyd or another IDG executive. "If there was an issue, he just didn't want to go there," said Carrigan. Instead, McGovern concentrated on building a strong team by embracing the positive kinds of reinforcement Norman Vincent Peale and Dale Carnegie espoused decades earlier.

"I spent a lot of time with Pat over the years," Carrigan said, "and the thing I learned most about him was his consistency, how he systematized his approach to running the company. Everything from his travels to all the cultural things he participated in. There was a rhythm that he established that was remarkable to see and required incredible personal energy and optimism."

For example, McGovern personally oversaw an annual four-day IDG leadership training session at an off-site retreat. The idea, Carrigan said, was to bring together about 25 of the company's best and brightest next generation of leaders to get a master class in the elements of IDG's business. Each year, McGovern would walk around the room, stop next to each participant, and talk about them and their accomplishments for the entire group to hear.

"He did it for everyone in the room," Carrigan said. "It took a really long time, and he never used any notes. He gave your history at the company, what you did before, said something funny about where you were from. It made people feel like a million bucks. The message was: 'I know you. I cared enough to learn about you. You are on my radar, and you are in the IDG family.'"

From the earliest days of the company, McGovern had the rare ability to find blue sky where others saw only rain. Few of his initial ideas were embraced by others in his orbit. In 1967, for example, the decision to publish a weekly computer newspaper was met with derision and scorn. There were so few computers out in the business world, there could hardly be enough news to fill a weekly paper. Undaunted and optimistic about his vision for the market, McGovern began to publish *Computerworld*, and within three years, he was putting out regular issues with 86 pages or more, 51 weeks a year. *Computerworld* became the largest business publication, in terms of both paid circulation and advertising dollars, in the country.

Computerworld's rise was not without serious challenges. Early in its infancy, Alan Taylor, the newspaper's founding editor, launched a surprise coup to take over the publication. Taylor believed that he had played a key role in the paper's early success and should have been rewarded by McGovern with a significant ownership stake. When this wasn't forthcoming, he complained to Walter Boyd about his feelings, but Boyd, confused by this aggressive stance, let it slide. Three months later, Taylor arrived at the publication's printer in Boston's Roxbury neighborhood ready to insert a front-page notice stating that he was now in charge of *Computerworld*. Boyd arrived at the printer before Taylor could initiate his takeover and demanded that Taylor cease and desist.

Boyd called Max Eveleth, an IDC employee who had played football at Dartmouth, and asked him to come to the printer and persuade Taylor to leave. The printer, unsure who to believe, said he would not print anything without talking to Pat McGovern, so the night ended in a stalemate. With McGovern out of the office and on the road, the situation turned into a bigger crisis the next day when Taylor stood up in the newsroom, announced he was taking over the publication, grabbed *Computerworld*'s financial ledgers, strong-armed Grace Polishook, the bookkeeper, to accompany him, and stormed out of the office. McGovern returned to Newton and called his lawyer, and Taylor, a talented but eccentric Brit, backed down.

Ironically, whereas most bosses would have been infuriated, pressed charges, and barred Taylor forever, McGovern took a different tack. He sat down and spoke to Taylor to iron out the differences, and invited Taylor to become a regular columnist for *Computerworld*. Taylor accepted and went on to become a highly visible, award-winning contributor to *Computerworld*. "Alan was a good, provocative columnist and understood the technology," said Drake Lundell, who served as *Computerworld*'s editor throughout the 1970s. McGovern undoubtedly realized the value that Taylor had brought to the publication and was enough of a savvy business leader to see that there was no upside to discarding an asset if you could find a way to make it work. "That was a very Pat thing to do," Lundell said.

There were other challenges. A painful recession in 1970 forced McGovern to scramble to save the fledgling company. The

Computerworld budget had to be cut by 20 percent, and the editorial department went to a four-day workweek to avoid massive layoffs. A line of credit from the First National Bank of Boston provided cash flow until things began to rebound. With his usual optimistic cheerleading, McGovern spearheaded a period of sustained growth for the publication and IDG. A short-term crisis was transformed into 20 years of unprecedented growth and profitability as *Computerworld* led IDG's worldwide expansion.

Jack Edmonston, who joined *Computerworld* in 1973 as an advertising salesman, remembers the heady early days, when the staff was crammed into a tiny office above a Chinese restaurant on Washington Street in Newton, Massachusetts, and *Computerworld* was growing fat with advertising. McGovern was intimately involved in every facet of the publication. He preached hiring great people and letting them do their thing, but in reality, this was his baby and he was driven to make sure it thrived. According to Edmonston, McGovern's belief in his vision inspired him to make *Computerworld* a paid rather than controlled circulation publication. It was a risky and audacious move. Most of the competitors in the trade press were controlled (i.e., free) publications, and by opting for a paid circulation, McGovern was able to quickly overtake its competitors in advertising sales. He never forgot the advice he had received from Lou Rader, the CEO of Univac, who told him that prospective customers were likely to assume something had real value if you charged more rather than less for it. That tenet was the foundation of McGovern's first foray into publishing, and it stuck with him. By 1970, even with the recession, *Computerworld* had 60,000 paid subscribers compared to 100,000 controlled subscribers for *Datamation*. By being more controversial, more timely, and news oriented, and by selling its industry knowledge generated by IDC, *Computerworld* rose to the pinnacle of the market.

According to Edmonston, *Computerworld*'s success was due mostly to McGovern's unwavering optimism and belief in his vision, sticking with his ideas for a long period of time despite losses and setbacks. And there were setbacks.

For example, soon after launching *Computerworld*, McGovern turned his attention to the Computer Caravan, a rolling technology exhibition, designed to travel to 10 US cities in 10 weeks as well as several in Europe. At the time, the two big computer conferences were the Spring Joint Computer Conference and the Fall Joint Computer Conference, which later merged to become the National Computer Conference (NCC). McGovern noticed that a majority of the attendees at these conferences came from local organizations. He believed there was an opportunity for a traveling conference that would be truly national in scope.

"We thought in 1970, with the recession in the industry, that the industry needed a real stimulus," McGovern said in an interview. "We said 'Let's find a way to bring the buyers in each of the major cities together with the industries so that they had better dialogue and could build the market.' We decided to do a trade show that went to ten cities in ten weeks."

McGovern spearheaded the new effort with enthusiasm, even climbing aboard a camel to promote the caravan concept. But without a deep understanding of the trade show landscape, problems quickly arose. "We didn't know too much about the trade show business. It sounded very simple to do. It turned out to be a logistical nightmare," McGovern recalled.

It was indeed a daunting task. IDG had to build the prefabricated booths and move them from convention center to convention center using a fleet of trailer trucks. It was winter and there were snowstorms and whiteouts, and the challenges began to outweigh the potential rewards. IDG invested $4 million to make the Computer Caravan a success, but it never found an audience. While most CEOs would lament the failed effort, McGovern saw the Computer Caravan through rose-colored glasses.

"We pride ourselves that we arranged about ten marriages during the course of this cycle," he recalled in the same interview. "People spending ten weeks in some of the best hotels around the country somehow led to some relationships that were enduring. We have about 25 Caravan children."

(Photo by J. Mourreau)

Computerworld Publisher Patrick McGovern leads the Computer Caravan to Boston.

Caravan to Begin in Boston

By a CW Staff Writer

BOSTON – With an expanded user program and 50% more exhibiting companies than last year, *Computerworld* officials are making last-minute preparations for the Computer Caravan, which begins its 10-city tour here next week.

Wilder, national sales manager for the caravan.

Additionally, five panel discussions, 11 workshops and a tutorial on data communications planning will be conducted in each city.

McGovern astride a camel in 1973 to promote the Computer Caravan trade show.

But McGovern was no Pollyanna. His optimism was heavily tempered with pragmatism, all in the determined effort to build and sustain the IDG empire.

Years later, for example, when Colin Crawford was CEO of Macworld, IDG's Apple-focused magazine and trade show, he faced the difficult challenge of a sullied Apple. McGovern and David Bunnell, a major figure in technology publishing, launched Macworld for IDG on the same day in 1984 that Steve Jobs unveiled the revolutionary Macintosh computer. The publication and the attendant trade show, produced by IDG World Expo, thrived as long as Apple did well. But Jobs was fired in 1985, and by the mid-1990s, much had changed and Apple's fortunes dipped. The iconic firm's market share began slipping dramatically and, with Steve Jobs gone and John Sculley being eased out as CEO, there were rumors flying that Apple's only recourse was to be acquired by IBM, Sun Microsystems, or Oracle. Hard as it is to imagine in today's market in which Apple is among the world's most valuable companies, Apple was in deep trouble. Its stock had tumbled, and Crawford realized that he had to downsize expectations for the publication.

Debut issue of *Macworld* in 1984.

"That was probably the hardest time and the hardest dealings I had with Pat because Pat was the eternal optimist," Crawford recalled. "Pat's graph only went in one direction, and it was usually exponential, so I had to sit down with Pat and explain to him that the storm clouds really were gathering, and it was up to us to manage what was probably going to be a difficult time."

Not surprisingly, McGovern insisted that Crawford was being too pessimistic. IDG published *Macworlds* all over the globe, and McGovern believed the market would rebound. Crawford explained that the publication along with the Macworld conference could still remain profitable, but not quite at the previous levels. McGovern had a steely resolve to focus on consistent growth. He would never raise his voice, but he always made clear to division leaders that they had to reach for the stars when it came to profits and growth. You couldn't rest on your laurels, and you couldn't achieve IDG-level success if you didn't have stretch goals. IDG's profit margins were among the highest in the industry, and he wanted to keep it that way.

Crawford was floored by what happened next. Rather than wait for the market to dictate Apple's fortunes, McGovern reached out to his competitor and nemesis Ziff Davis to suggest a merger of Mac publications. Ziff Davis, a fierce challenger in the technology media space, had emerged in the 1980s as the main rival when it shifted its focus from such hobbyist magazines as *Popular Aviation* and *Car and Driver* to the emerging technology marketplace. The competition had heated up in 1982 when William Ziff, the company's dynamic chairman and CEO, acquired *PC Magazine* out from under McGovern, who thought he had a deal in place for the up-and-coming publication. McGovern retaliated by recruiting David Bunnell, the founder of *PC Magazine*, to come to IDG to create *PCWorld* and *Macworld* magazines.

Ziff Davis began to publish a series of titles in direct competition with many of IDG's publications, including *MacUser* and *Macweek*, and had its own unique culture of winning at all costs. McGovern felt no love lost for Bill Ziff, though the two men shared much in common. Ziff was "a polymath with a photographic memory," according to the *New York Times*, a description that fit McGovern as well.[2] Eventually, they came to a grudging respect for each other, but it was a tenuous truce. At its height in the 1980s and '90s, these were the two giants of the technology media publishing universe, and the rivalry was heated. Having been diagnosed with terminal prostate cancer many years earlier, Bill Ziff decided to sell Ziff Davis in 1994 to Forstmann Little, but he maintained a presence in the firm. Three years later, when McGovern suggested the Mac merger, the competitive juices were still very much in evidence.

The two companies were cultural opposites—Ziff Davis was an intense sales- and marketing-driven culture, while IDG tended to be more familial and editorial- and research-driven—and the battles for readership across many common market publications was legendary. So for McGovern to reach out to Ziff to merge Apple titles was a shocking move.

For Crawford, the joint venture was a formidable challenge, given Apple's sagging fortunes in 1997. He didn't believe a joint venture made sense, and he felt that Ziff's *MacUser* was actually ready to fold. He recalled that Pat had negotiated a merger in the 1980s of IDG's early Apple II publication *InCider* with Ziff's *A+* magazine, and he believed that experience must have prompted McGovern to forge this new deal.

Despite all the market challenges, however, the joint venture proved successful, though Ziff Davis ultimately reaped a $20 million haul when IDG bought Ziff's 50 percent stake in 2001. While IDG owned the Mac publication market, tensions between Jobs, who had returned to run Apple in 1997, and McGovern grew. Jobs had long been simmering over his decision to grant IDG rights to the Mac name back in 1984, and he was especially furious when IDG decided to move the Macworld Expo from New York to Boston. Jobs told Crawford, "I don't play Off Broadway!" and refused to support the move. He did, however, remain committed to the Macworld Expo in San Francisco.

"I believe Pat saw the joint venture through rose-tinted spectacles," Crawford said. "He believed he could drive prices in the market. He was always pushing the premium model: high CPMs, high subscription and newsstand prices. His supreme optimism made him believe that IDG would be able to generate higher returns because IDG's model was better than the one deployed by Ziff."

Once again, McGovern's vision proved accurate over the long haul. As Apple's fortunes rebounded after Jobs returned to run the company, the Macworld Expo in San Francisco became a hugely profitable business for IDG, in part because Steve Jobs announced many of Apple's signature products of the new millennium—most prominently, the iPhone in 2007—at the event. *Macworld* magazine became the premier source of news and information about Apple and its vaunted product line.

"At its best, [*Macworld*] may have been the finest magazine about one specific computing platform that anyone's ever published—well written, beautifully designed, and surprisingly provocative," wrote Harry McCracken, technology editor at *Fast Company* and a former IDG editor, in 2014 when IDG ceased the print version of *Macworld*.[3] Today, Macworld is an online publication only, but it remains the leading Apple publication on the market.

BRAIN OPTIMISM

There's not much that cries optimism more than a $350 million gift to a university to create a major world-class research center. When McGovern and his wife, Lore, decided in the mid-1990s to fund an institute to explore and research the mysteries and intricacies of the human brain, McGovern was optimistic that this research would lead to a better and safer world for all human beings.

"I felt in the beginning of the 1990s that the development of super high-speed computers really could make neural network modeling effective," McGovern said in an interview in 2000. "Now the tools are really available to make some major advances in understanding how the brain receives information, analyzes it, understands it, stores it, retrieves it, and prepares it for recommunication."

From the outset, McGovern embraced his new legacy, the McGovern Institute for Brain Research (MIBR), with a positive fervor that felt like the earliest days of IDG. This was deeply important to him, and he had no doubt that the lab would become a centerpiece in the global attempt to understand the human brain. He and Lore attended seminars, took notes, asked questions, and understood viscerally what was going on.

"Pat would act like an assistant professor who thought eventually he was going to come up for tenure," said Robert Desimone, the director of the MIBR. "They both asked a lot of questions, and showed they were really committed. So people regarded him as a colleague in a way. The faculty really appreciated that."

McGovern brought his well-traveled business philosophy to the lab. Give great people the resources and let them take control of their own efforts, and this will yield the best results, whether in the office or the research lab. At the same time, like at IDG, he kept a close eye on the leadership and direction of the center, believing that a personal touch is essential to success.

He said he learned from talking to other philanthropists of the importance of "acting early on whatever dream you have to contribute your resources back to society. You want to have an active voice in the way in which your resources are used to fulfill the dream you have. A lot of philanthropists have waited too late in their life, and by the time they are making their donation, they are at an age in life where their physical and mental energy really doesn't give them much ability to provide leadership on the use of their resources."

Philip Sharp, the MIBR's founding director and a Nobel laureate in medicine, stepped down after five years, and Desimone took over as director. He said the leaders at the MIBR used to joke that McGovern saw the center as just another business unit of IDG.

"We operated independently, to a large extent," Desimone said. "We had tremendous autonomy, but Pat provided a general oversight and philosophy and encouragement. And as long as things were going well, he didn't want to interfere in any way. He encouraged us to set high standards and a high bar for success."

McGovern was so optimistic about the promise of brain research that he also set up the research institutes in China and had plans to open others around the world. His untimely death put those plans on indefinite hold.

"A lot of people who donate money have done so because they have family health issues," Desimone explained. "They've had somebody in the family who has suffered from a severe mental illness or brain injury, and that is certainly a good reason for them to offer support. But Pat and Lore didn't have that as a motivation. It was really the excitement about brain research and the fact that it was ultimately going to help other people that was important to them."

McGovern's unmatched enthusiasm and the faculty response created a collegial and invigorating atmosphere that turned the new lab into a desired destination for top researchers. Its reputation spread, and when the center was recruiting talented researchers to join the ranks, they would hear from faculty how much people loved working there. "It had a really big impact," Desimone stated.

Pat McGovern at the MIBR with actor Alan Alda and producer Graham Chedd for the PBS documentary *Brains on Trial*.

Of course, the pragmatic side never disappeared from the equation. This wasn't unlimited positive love; McGovern had expectations, and his support had to be earned. Deliverables were put in place and milestones set along the way. His ultimate wish was for the emergence of life-changing ideas and therapies, the translation of basic research into breakthrough clinical applications.

"There is an appreciation that you can't have translational neuroscience if there's nothing to translate, and that is really critical for us," Desimone said. "You've got to build a strong foundation if you want to come up with the things that will ultimately help people. You can't bypass the foundation."

If it sounds familiar, it is a philosophy that pervaded all that McGovern touched. "The faith that positive outcomes will occur is critical to the philosophy of the McGovern Institute," Desimone added, "and that's the way Pat thought."

TAKEAWAYS

▶▶ Regardless of setbacks and rough times, McGovern remained an unfettered optimist. His signature: "The best is yet to come."

▶▶ Optimism is an asset to the bottom line.

▶▶ For visionary leaders, optimism is a required trait that inspires good people to work harder and achieve more.

LESSON SEVEN
Integrity Is Priceless: Never Cross the Line in the Sand

If people like you, they'll listen to you, but if they trust you, they'll do business with you.
—ZIG ZIGLAR,
salesman and motivational speaker

"Pat had your back."

Speak to editors and reporters who worked at IDG publications over the decades, and that is the common refrain. From his earliest days in the business, McGovern hired talented people, gave them the resources to do their jobs, and assured them that editorial integrity was sacrosanct. It was the formula for achieving high editorial quality, building respected individual brands, and developing a massive global media company.

Covering an industry as volatile and fast-growing as information technology was lucrative but filled with minefields. Vendors who advertised in IDG publications were quick to push back against negative coverage, often threatening to pull advertising and identifying editors with whom they had bones to pick. The trade press, across countless vertical industries, had a reputation for porous borders between editorial and advertising. Unlike the mainstream business press, trade publications were often counted on by some of the heavy hitters like IBM or Microsoft or Apple to repress bad news and publish flattering fluff.

For Pat McGovern, the decision about the separation of church and state (editorial and advertising) was simple: Product quality and integrity were the hallmarks of IDG's brand, and if he allowed advertisers to dictate the kind of coverage they got, the brand would be tarnished, bereft of any semblance of credibility in readers' eyes. As the technology industry burgeoned, McGovern knew he had to respect his readers or they'd abandon IDG's lineup of publications. He set the line deeply and indelibly in the sand and never wavered in supporting his editorial staffs. McGovern was an erstwhile journalist at heart, having served as an editor for his high school and college newspapers. He was working as a professional editor and reporter when he founded IDG. In publishing, he believed, editorial integrity was the corporate oxygen. It was a leadership lesson he passed on to his legion of editorial employees.

McGovern knew the intricacies of media policy and the value of integrity. It was a tenet he lived by throughout his career, and though he left a lot of advertising money on the table over the years by backing his editorial staffs, he remained confident that he had a good product and a vast audience, and the advertisers would come back. Inevitably, they did.

In the early days of *Computerworld*, for example, NCR, a major computer maker in that era, paid for the first-ever two-page, full-color spread in the publication. It was a major advertising coup for the *Computerworld* sales staff, and they were more than a bit nonplussed when the issue appeared with a front-page article whose headline blared: "NCR Tape Drives Crash." McGovern didn't blink or swallow hard. He understood the trade-off and stood firm behind editorial independence. "There was never any pandering," Walter Boyd said. "It was impossible to bribe him in any way, shape, or form."

Boyd described a call IDG received in 1969 from IBM headquarters. A group from IBM was coming from White Plains to Boston, and they thought it would be in McGovern's best interest to meet for dinner at Locke-Ober, a landmark Boston eatery. McGovern invited Boyd to join him, and when they arrived, they were ushered into a private room IBM had arranged. There were eight IBMers, Boyd recalled, two product managers, and the rest, lawyers. Their mission was to coerce McGovern into changing the company name. They said IDC (the company's name before switching to IDG) was too close to IBM and was confusing people. IBM was facing a significant market shift at the time. The unbundling of hardware, software, and peripherals was just getting under way, and users found they no longer had to buy everything from IBM. This was costing IBM market share, and Big Blue was aggressive about protecting its vast turf.

McGovern calmly responded that he liked the name IDC, and he planned to make the company international someday. Upon leaving the meeting, he turned to Boyd and said, "That was a nice meal." Though he later received follow-up letters with veiled threats, he was unmoved. "Nothing ever bowed Pat," Boyd said. "He was pretty fearless. He had ideas of what he was going to do and how he was going to do it, and the devil take the hindmost."

In fact, in the late 1960s, *Computerworld* aggressively covered the trial when IBM became embroiled in a major antitrust case. Drake Lundell, editor of *Computerworld* during that period, recalled that the corporate data processing managers who made up a large percentage of *Computerworld*'s readers "were pretty much under the control of IBM, and we regularly pointed out that IBM and its pricing policies were screwing them over."

The government and several rival companies, such as Telex, took the same view, and in 1969, filed antitrust charges against Big Blue. Lundell pointed out that *Computerworld* was the only publication that covered the Telex vs. IBM trial in Tulsa, and it was during that trial that detailed internal IBM documents regarding their pricing policies became public.

"Rather than being an industry supporter and cheerleader, *Computerworld* in many ways was probably the first consumer-oriented publication," Lundell said, suggesting that *Computerworld* was, in some ways, the *Consumer Reports* of the technology industry.

Computerworld began extensive coverage of the IBM antitrust case, even going so far as to send Edie Holmes, one of its top reporters, to New York to report on the trial on a daily basis from the Second District Courthouse. IDG rented an apartment on Tenth Street where Holmes could stay while the trial was in session. For long stretches, Holmes was the only reporter in the courtroom every day. *Computerworld* even installed a Teletype machine in the apartment so Holmes could produce a daily roundup of the trial proceedings, which the company offered on a subscription basis to law firms and other interested companies.

As the 8,000-pound gorilla in the IT industry, IBM was a crucial advertiser for the publication, and IBM executives were not pleased with *Computerworld*'s laser focus on the trial. McGovern was summoned to IBM's Armonk headquarters on more than one occasion, but he refused to budge on the paper's coverage, despite threats to pull advertising. "He didn't even break a sweat," Boyd recalled. "He was not intimidated."

IBM became fixated on *Computerworld*'s coverage. The paper was printed in Chicago on Thursday nights, so it could be delivered via the mail on Monday morning to most of its readers. IBM sent one of its Chicago-based employees to the printing plant to purloin early copies of the publication. "Twice, when I was editor, I received calls on Friday morning from IBMers complaining about stories in the paper to be delivered on Monday," Lundell recalled. "One was from [IBM CEO] Frank Cary himself. He was upset about a story about some shady IBM practices in South America. He didn't contest the facts, but he said we shouldn't have published it in the national interest!"

Lundell was also called to IBM's headquarters in Armonk. "They showed me their rating system for *Computerworld* stories," he explained. "They judged *every paragraph* of a story as positive (+), negative (–), or neutral (=) and came up with an overall grade for every story that mentioned IBM. Talk about anal retentive." Lundell noted that most of the stories received neutral ratings because *Computerworld* ran a lot of stories about customers who were doing interesting things with IBM technology. But most of those stories were "back of the book, and our front-page stuff really set them off."

Years later, when Thomas Watson Jr., the legendary IBM CEO, was honored with a *Computerworld*/Smithsonian Lifetime Achievement Award in Washington, Watson spoke about the adversarial relationship that had developed between IBM and IDG. But he paid McGovern the ultimate compliment. "We cringed at what they were writing about us," Watson told the audience, "but we couldn't afford not to read it because it was the bible of the industry." It was McGovern's dogged belief in editorial integrity that fueled the coverage and set the tone for IDG's growing stable of publications.

When McGovern convinced Bob Metcalfe, the inventor of Ethernet and cofounder of 3Com, to join *InfoWorld* in 1991, Metcalfe began writing a column for the publication. In one of his early pieces, Metcalfe "savaged" Hewlett-Packard for calling one of its networking products Ethernet when it really wasn't Ethernet. "I had a special interest in that," Metcalfe said.

The day after it was published, Metcalfe got a call from an HP spokesperson informing him that the company had cancelled advertising in *all* IDG publications as a result of his column. Having been on the job for just a few months, Metcalfe was not prepared for such an extreme response. He reluctantly called McGovern and explained what had happened. McGovern responded: "Well, I read your column and it looked pretty good to me. Don't worry. They'll be back because they need us."

A week later, the "adult supervision" at HP, as Metcalfe called it, took over, and they reinstated their advertising contracts with IDG. "One of Pat's wonderful features was that he walked the talk, and one of his talks was the separation of church and state,"

Metcalfe said. "Advertising and editorial were kept separate. As the publisher, I wasn't even allowed on the seventh floor, which was the editorial floor. Pat didn't go anywhere near reprimanding me for my column. He just insisted that church and state be separate."

Bill Laberis, who became editor in chief of *Computerworld* in 1986, was nervous about taking on such a high-level position without prior experience as the top editor. When he took the job, *Computerworld* had been struggling as the technology marketplace began shifting. The advent of personal computing was already grabbing industry headlines, but *Computerworld*, with its focus on IT professionals in corporate settings, was missing the revolution. Laberis faced the challenge of righting the listing ship while learning on the job. McGovern immediately set Laberis's mind at ease.

On one of his first visits from McGovern, Laberis was told he would have whatever resources he needed and free rein to get *Computerworld* running on all cylinders. "He sat down and said, 'You are head of the most important publication we have, so anything you need, just tell my office, and we'll get you what you want to succeed. You need to make sure you put out a wonderful and unbiased publication week after week.'"

Laberis took the promise seriously, and for 10 years, he felt McGovern had his back. When Laberis was offered the coveted position of publisher in 1991, he shocked everyone by turning down the lucrative opportunity. "I had the best job in the world," he explained. "I had a large staff. I could meet with anybody in the industry I wanted to see. Pat talked to me about having not taken the publisher's job and told me he respected my decision." Given what Laberis had sacrificed to stay in his position, the decision to remain on the editorial side of the aisle was significant within IDG's hierarchy.

Throughout his tenure, Laberis had a somewhat contentious relationship with *Computerworld*'s sales managers. There was a lot of push and pull about coverage, and he always insisted on maintaining the wall between editorial and advertising. The salespeople were not shy about trying to influence editorial even though they were well aware of McGovern's edicts. Laberis knew McGovern was behind him. "Pat never wavered in his respect for editorial integrity," he said.

For example, when he was hired, Laberis inherited a tense relationship with one of *Computerworld*'s major advertisers, Computer Associates. CA is a large, independent systems software provider, and in those days, a formidable player in the mainframe software marketplace. Its founder and CEO, Charles Wang, was a tough, smart, and aggressive leader who kept a close eye on coverage of his company. He had very thin skin when it came to perceived knocks on CA. *Computerworld* had a reporter assigned to cover CA, and the company was a highly visible source of stories that spawned an endless stream of headlines.[1]

Wang dissected each issue, and if there were stories about the company that didn't reflect what he wanted to see, especially some that mentioned dissatisfaction among CA customers, he would threaten to pull advertising and often did. And then he would come back. Major technology players couldn't afford to be absent from the pages of *Computerworld* for any length of time.

Gary Beach, who took the publisher's position at *Computerworld*, had also heard from Wang. When Laberis was invited to meet Wang in his office, Wang told him he had secured a promise from Beach and then IDG CEO Kelly Conlin that all stories about CA would be reviewed by Beach before being published. Laberis stayed calm but replied, "That isn't going to happen." The meeting ended on a cordial note, but the dustup was hardly finished. Not surprising, this promise caused some friction between Laberis and Beach.

Beach acknowledged it was difficult for those on the business side "because editors felt they could go right to Pat." He had to contend with Wang's harangues as well but found little sympathy from McGovern. "Pat said to me one day, 'I can assess the editorial value of IDG publications by how many times I get sued each year,' " Beach recalled.

Laberis sent a memo to the entire editorial staff, including reporters, copy editors, and section editors, making clear that no such reviews of stories would take place outside the editorial office. The tension grew worse. At the next quarterly meeting, which McGovern attended, the issue was raised. Word of the conflict had already gotten to him. At the meeting, he made a point of addressing it very publicly to everyone in the room. He said, "We have the best editor in the world and the best staff. They will take care of everything editorially." Beach, needless to say, was not happy. He had to back off the promise he had made to Wang to personally vet each *Computerworld* story about CA.

"It was a real Pat moment," Laberis said. "He knew once we lost our editorial integrity, we'd lose everything."

The impact on Laberis was profound. When a reporter would promise to "nail" a company in an article, Laberis took him off the story. Integrity had to work both ways. Reporters couldn't go into an assignment with an attitude or preexisting bias. As information technology was becoming more of a game-changing factor in corporations, the mainstream business media like *Businessweek*, the *Wall Street Journal*, *Fortune*, and the *New York Times* began to increase their coverage. Trade journalists who could explain the burgeoning phenomenon were being recruited by these publications. Because it was so financially successful, *Computerworld* had the luxury of sticking to its guns. It was the only computer industry publication with a paid subscription base. Due to that, its pass-along readership soared to more than 400,000 readers per week. Competitors had to print that many issues and give them away.

"Our success hinged on us knocking it out of the park with independent research studies," Laberis said. McGovern believed that editorial integrity, more than anything else, drove the paper's financial success for so many years. It was why editors could lose their job if they crossed the line.

With his platform secure, Laberis made two more visits to Long Island to see Charles Wang. He promised to look at all CA stories before they ran, which was something he did anyway. But it swayed Wang that Laberis would be a better friend than enemy, so he backed off. In fact, over time, the two formed a strong professional relationship based on mutual respect. Wang even asked Laberis to give the keynote at a CA user conference in New Orleans. "This was all because Pat trusted me to work things out myself," Laberis recalled. "He supported me even when his top people went in a different direction."

STEVE JOBS ON THE LINE

Given IDG's prominent role in advancing the surging importance of information technology during the 1970s and 1980s, it was inevitable that McGovern would cross paths with Steve Jobs, Apple's volatile chief executive. IDG didn't just find new geographies to conquer, it focused on new technology platforms as well. And in 1984, when Jobs introduced his breakthrough Macintosh computer, IDG published a new magazine called *Macworld* on the day the product shipped. McGovern and David Bunnell, the editor and founder of *PCWorld*, convinced Jobs to license the Macintosh name to IDG and to advertise in the new publication. IDG would also organize the Macworld Expo in San Francisco, which gave Jobs the perfect platform from which to announce his parade of new products. More than anything, Jobs wanted people's attention, and a publication and trade show devoted to his exciting new product helped generate that audience.

It isn't clear when he came to regret licensing the name, but for an iconoclast like Jobs, who required complete control of his world, the relationship with IDG quickly became an irritant. He was unhappy that others were making money off Apple's success.

"He hated that IDG made a successful business of *Macworld* and the Macworld Expo," said Jason Snell, who served as editor of *Macworld* for 10 years before becoming an independent writer and podcaster. "He regretted licensing the name to IDG. Leave aside that it greatly benefitted Apple for years and created the keynote as we know it to this day. You could tell this was how he felt. He believed that Pat and IDG built itself on the greatness of companies like Apple."

Publicly, he and McGovern refrained from criticizing each other. But privately, the relationship was a bit less circumspect. A certain level of tension grew between the two and would come to a head two decades later when Jobs decided to pull out of the Macworld Expo.

But in the summer of 1985, when Jobs was ousted by Apple's board in favor of new CEO John Sculley, *Macworld* magazine continued its attempt to build an audience.[2] The Macintosh computer found a growing fan base, and the publication grew significantly into the 1990s, reaching $30 million in revenue by 1994. But in those days, the company's market share was low, and its products started losing additional ground to the dominant Microsoft Windows–based offerings.

Jobs spent time feeling angry and vengeful, and then, rejuvenated, he focused his efforts on NeXT, his new venture, which was an attempt to enter the workstation marketplace. In 1991, in a gesture of respect and admiration for his talents, McGovern immediately funded the creation of *NeXTworld*, a magazine for that prospective audience. Instead of gratitude, Jobs called McGovern to complain about the editorial coverage and suggested the editor of *NeXTworld* be fired on the spot. McGovern, of course, refused, and Jobs was left to fume over what he perceived as a tremendous slight.

"Steve always had an attitude that the media was there to be at his beck and call, and to write nice things about his shiny new toys," said Colin Crawford, who had become CEO of *Macworld* in 1993. As Apple's fortunes sagged, Sculley was forced out by the board and things continued to get worse. Rumors abounded about the survival of the iconic firm. But when then Apple CEO Gil Amelio decided to acquire NeXT for $400 million, Jobs returned to Apple, engineered a coup to remove Amelio, and found himself in charge of his beloved company once again. What Jobs did at Apple became industry legend. He quickly jump-started the company, but he was no less prickly and contentious with the media.[3]

In his role at *Macworld*, Crawford became IDG's main liaison to Apple and to Jobs. Jobs routinely called Crawford with complaints about editorial and advertising issues. Over time, Crawford came to dread calls from Jobs, usually late at night at home, because "he was not calling me up to see how my family was doing," Crawford recalled.

After the introduction of Apple's iMac laptop computer, for example, Crawford decided to launch a subsidiary publication called *iMacworld* that was meant to cover the entry-level marketplace. It was a test to see if there really was a business there. Crawford visited Apple, discussed his plans with several executives, and received no objections to the concept.

But then his home phone rang at 10 p.m. It was Jobs. "Colin," he said, "we've got a problem. You've stolen our trademark. I hear you are launching a new publication called *iMacworld*, and you know, we own the mark iMac. Years ago, we made the mistake of licensing Mac to IDG, and that is something I've regretted for the last 10 years. So we're definitely not licensing the iMac mark to anyone."

Crawford tried to explain that he would just print an "I" before *Macworld,* and Jobs started to laugh. "You know how this is going to go down, Colin, don't you?" said Jobs with some menace to his tone. In the end, Crawford and IDG backed off and killed the new publication, unwilling to fight the battle for a noncritical business decision.

Over the years, Crawford managed to develop a working relationship with Jobs, an unusual rapport for someone with Jobs's disdain for the media. Knowing the tension between Jobs and McGovern, Crawford, when asked if he had occasion to bring the pair together in a room, replied, "Part of my job was to make sure that happened as little as possible."

Though both were highly successful entrepreneurs, their personalities were poles apart. Whereas McGovern was a warm and embracing presence who greeted each stranger with a smile and welcoming handshake, Jobs, according to Crawford, was dismissive of most people, especially women. He called McGovern's Silicon Valley home on occasion, and if Lore, McGovern's wife, answered, he made no small talk. If McGovern wasn't at home, he hung up quickly. He did the same to Crawford's wife when he called their home.

But given IDG's stake in the *Macworld* franchise, Crawford was determined to keep Jobs placated as much as possible. Not everyone at IDG understood the complex and volatile Jobs like Crawford did. In 2000, during the first dot-com boom, IDG's newly formed Internet sales group decided to place a billboard touting its Internet prowess along Highway 101 in the heart of Silicon Valley. Apple had recently launched its "Think Different" ad campaign. Someone at IDG decided it would be fun to put up an ad with a stern-looking Jobs lookalike and the tagline "Think Differently. Think IDG."

Taunting Steve Jobs was never a good idea. Three days after the billboard went up, Crawford got a call from an Apple marketing executive suggesting he arrange to take it down. Crawford replied, "I can't do anything. It's outside my jurisdiction. It has nothing to do with me."

Days later, another Apple executive called and said, "We've got a relationship with you. Maybe you can help deal with this." Again Crawford explained it was not his decision. And then, two days later, Katie Cotton, Apple's head of public relations, called and said, "Steve wants to talk to you." She handed the phone to Jobs, who minced no words.

"Colin, you know that billboard? Every day, Larry Ellison, who by the way, is my best friend, drives past that billboard, and every time he passes it, he picks up his car phone, speed-dials me, and tells me I'm an idiot for allowing that thing to stay up." Crawford waited. "I know it's outside your jurisdiction," Jobs added, "but I don't give a damn if you have to go out there with a chainsaw and take it down yourself. You've got 48 hours and that thing has to disappear.

"You know I don't make idle threats," Jobs railed on. "If you want to continue any form of business relationship between IDG and Apple, you better talk to the right people."

Crawford called IDG CEO Kelly Conlin and explained the situation. "Doesn't Steve have a sense of humor?" Conlin asked. But he got the message and the billboard came down.

In 2007, Crawford moved from *Macworld* to become CEO of *PCWorld*. Just a couple of months into his new role, he encountered a firestorm that reflected his fraught and stressful relationship with Jobs.

On a Friday afternoon at *PCWorld*'s San Francisco office, a marketing person nervously knocked on his door and handed him a press release slated to go out from the editorial department on Monday. She'd received a note from the magazine's managing editor who was anxious to promote an article in the upcoming issue. The story was entitled "Ten Things We Hate About Apple." It was part of a package that included a companion piece "Ten Things We Love About Apple."

Like *Macworld*, *PCWorld* also covered Apple, which was driving a record run of game-changing product introductions and rampaging sales. Crawford asked for a copy of the story and saw what he thought was a sophomoric attempt at humor—"We hate Steve because he dresses in turtlenecks and doesn't change his jeans"—and for him, one that simply prodded the bear, a bear with whom he was quite familiar. His immediate reaction was that the piece did not service the magazine's mission, which was to provide product advice to readers.

New to his job, Crawford was sensitive about *PCWorld*'s difficult financial position and the declining print market, and he knew that Apple and Jobs were looking for any excuse to distance themselves further from IDG, especially related to Macworld Expo. "I figured, if this hits, we'll be getting a call from Apple saying, 'We're outta here!'" Crawford said.

Crawford knew McGovern highly valued the Apple relationship. Crawford had negotiated a handshake deal with Jobs back in

1997 that Apple would take the inside advertising spreads in each issue of *Macworld*. There was no formal contract. Even though *Macworld* remained editorially independent, it was good for both organizations to continue to support the Mac market. Apple was also advertising in *PCWorld*, and IDG needed assurance that an Apple executive, preferably Jobs, would appear on stage at the Macworld Expo. In January 2007, Jobs had introduced the iPhone at Macworld, and it was a watershed moment in tech industry history. Without Jobs on stage, the show would fizzle.

With all that in mind, Crawford made a snap decision. "It can't run," he declared, effectively killing the story. He called Harry McCracken, editor of *PCWorld* and a respected veteran tech journalist. McCracken was on an airplane and didn't get Crawford's agitated call. So Crawford pushed ahead and typed an e-mail to McCracken telling him the story wouldn't run. Crawford checked with Kevin Krull, IDG's in-house counsel, who agreed with his decision.

McCracken, an editor with a spotless reputation in his 15 years at IDG, received Crawford's e-mail, and he immediately pushed back. The article was an unedited draft, he replied, and could be tweaked to make it less volatile, but he had a serious problem with the president of the business unit dictating editorial decisions.

"I didn't think the president and CEO should decide what we should run," McCracken said. "Colin didn't see it as something open to negotiation. He said there could be catastrophic consequences for IDG. I proposed various solutions, and he wouldn't talk about it. So I decided to quit."

Crawford was disappointed, but he didn't try to dissuade McCracken. There was no yelling or angry debate, but McCracken knew he couldn't live with this breach of editorial independence.

When word reached the *PCWorld* staff, anger erupted. One or two staffers immediately shared the news with friends at tech media websites, and the story began to go viral. The pundits who followed the world of tech journalism at outlets such as *Wired* magazine and CNET were all over it. Stories about the incident written by former IDG employees appeared, and the *PCWorld* editorial staff grew more furious. Crawford spoke to the staff and tried to calm them down, but he failed to gain any backing. An outsider, Crawford wasn't likely to get the benefit of the doubt from a staff already wary of his presence.

He also tried to convince McCracken to return, but McCracken felt that this issue struck at the heart of IDG's editorial integrity, something for which McGovern and generations of IDG journalists felt great pride.

Events unfolded quickly for Crawford. He got strong support from some members of the IDG executive team, and he believed McGovern was sympathetic but was stuck between a rock and a hard place. McGovern's career-long support of editorial independence was being put to the test, and when the story took on a life of its own, he had to publicly make a choice. An innocuous situation was getting ugly. Bloggers posted cartoons of a heroic McCracken on a horse slaying a capitalistic monster with Crawford's face. When an article about the dustup appeared in the *New York Times*, Crawford saw the handwriting on the wall.[4]

As the kerfuffle escalated, McCracken felt uneasy but determined. He had no interest in hurting the company's reputation—he had long felt great loyalty and affection for IDG—but he had his own reputation to consider. Bob Carrigan, then president of IDG, tried to intervene to no avail. Finally, McGovern reached out directly to McCracken. He left McCracken a simple phone message: "When it comes to editorial content, you don't work for the president of *PCWorld*. You make the final call."

"That meant a lot to me," McCracken said. McGovern rarely had to get involved in such disputes, but this time, the surging publicity was creating a mountain out of what would have been a molehill of a story. The Apple articles were meant to be a lighthearted jab at the company, not the vicious attack that Crawford believed it to be. McCracken told Carrigan he would return if Crawford stepped down. The damage had been done, and Crawford decided he had no choice but to resign. "I knew it was time to move aside," he said. "Because once you start to question my governance, independence, and reputation, then we have to fall on our swords. There was nothing else to do." McGovern, as always, had followed his instincts about the sanctity of editorial.

But McGovern was never comfortable losing talented managers, and he was unwilling to jettison Crawford despite the controversy. In fact, after resigning, Crawford flew to Beijing to honor a previous commitment to make a presentation at an IDG managers meeting. When he arrived at that evening's dinner reception, McGovern headed straight for him. "I didn't know what to expect," Crawford said, "but he greeted me warmly and asked me to sit with him at dinner. That action spoke a thousand words for me."

McGovern suggested Crawford return to a corporate business development position within IDG, and Crawford agreed. Ironically, the resulting *PCWorld* article about Apple hardly made a ripple. It had been much ado about very little.[5]

The *New York Times* followed up on the story. "Who says industry magazines are cozy with their advertisers?" the article began. It went on to describe the "hero's homecoming" for McCracken and quoted readers who said they were about to cancel their subscriptions to the magazine before he returned. For McCracken, McGovern's support was extraordinary.

"Editors always knew that IDG and Pat had their back," McCracken recalled. "He was genuinely interested in the content produced by his company, and he was committed to editorial integrity. When it comes to editorial integrity, you can't get your virginity back. I had worked for publishers at magazines who barely knew what was in the content. Pat deeply imbued the company with the values that were important to him. As an editor, it was a huge deal to know the person in charge cared about this stuff."

TAKEAWAYS

▶▶ In any corporate setting, but especially in the media business, integrity is an unassailable asset and must be protected.

▶▶ The separation of church and state must be inviolate, and the leader must be prepared to enforce that corporate tenet, regardless of the cost.

▶▶ Not only does the brand benefit from staunch CEO support in this regard, but the best and brightest talent is attracted to an organization whose leader has their back.

▶▶ The savvy CEO understands how potent such empowerment is for his or her senior managers. Integrity flows down through such an organization.

9

LESSON EIGHT
"Loose-Tight" Leadership
Builds Empires

I don't believe in just ordering people to do things.
You have to sort of grab an oar and row with them.
—HAROLD S. GENEEN,
ITT

A s a young entrepreneur trying to manage a fast-growing company, Patrick McGovern was influenced by Harold Geneen, an outspoken iconoclast who took over International Telephone and Telegraph Corporation (ITT) in 1959 and built it into a massive global conglomerate. During his 18-year tenure, Geneen grew the company from under $800 million in sales to $17 billion. Through countless acquisitions, he entered a variety of industries and geographies.

In the late 1960s, Geneen was the Steve Jobs of his day, a brash, self-involved visionary who reconsidered conventional management wisdom and followed a different track to success. According to the *New York Times*, he was considered "the most significant and controversial businessman of the 1960's and 70's."[1] His theories were the subject of academic papers, dissected in business school classes, and he cowrote a bestselling book called *Managing* to share his wisdom. Though McGovern's style was vastly different from Geneen's, one could see aspects of Geneen's management philosophy in the nascent IDG.

Geneen embraced a "loose-tight" philosophy, a management structure that gave business units great autonomy and freedom but kept a tight fist around financial controls and accountability. It was an effective way to manage a huge, sprawling conglomerate, and it fit perfectly into McGovern's decentralized vision.

"You could see parts of Hal Geneen in McGovern's early philosophy because it was unlike IBM, which was very army, regimental, span of control kind of thinking," said Pat Kenealy. "Geneen kept the corporate staff lean, flew around all the time to see the operating units, audited them once or twice a year, but if they made their financial plan, he left them alone."

Geneen bought up businesses like most executives buy tailored dress shirts. During his reign, ITT acquired 350 companies in 80 countries including Avis Rent-a-Car and Sheraton Hotels. Unlike McGovern, who focused his full attention on information technology media, Geneen believed you could run any collection of businesses if you were a good manager. He bought companies that were countercyclical to those he already owned, and he focused on cash-flow businesses rather than asset businesses. He acquired both domestically and overseas, and he worked 70- to 80-hour weeks to stay on top of his empire.

Unlike Geneen, McGovern built his loose-tight culture based on his own sense of how best to treat employees, customers, and stakeholders. He preferred IDG to create its own businesses rather than acquire them, though he made many acquisitions over the years. Some flourished, some crashed and burned. He pushed the boundaries, but not as far as Geneen, who got ITT into trouble with accusations that he used bribes and payoffs in foreign markets to further his ends.

For McGovern, the lesson was clear: Be humble. Honor stakeholders, customers, and employees. Listen and learn. Make curiosity a driving business advantage. But never forget that someone has to have the final word. It takes courage and conviction to stand firm when necessary.

Leaders aiming to spawn the kind of productive, loyal, aggressive, and effective company that IDG became often rely on command and control tactics as a means to an end. GE chief Jack Welch became a legend for his "take-no-prisoners, fire-the-bottom-10-percent" approach. Steve Jobs, Martha Stewart, Henry Ford, and Leona Helmsley were autocratic leaders whose "Vlad the Impaler" management styles spawned various levels of success and failure.

Conversely, *servant leadership*, an ancient but timeless approach, relies on the selfless, introspective leader who inverts the pyramid, lets the bottom influence the top, and encourages a workforce to drive the business model. McGovern was a hybrid who drew on the best of both models to keep IDG moving profitably forward for nearly 50 years.

"He really practiced that servant leadership model," said Bob Carrigan. "He was 100 percent consistent, absolutely unflappable, possibly even too trusting. It didn't work perfectly every time, but it did the vast majority of the time. His formula, when he applied it, worked to incredible success."

MAKING DUMPLINGS

With his embrace of decentralization, entrusting local leaders around the globe, and encouraging every employee to come up with ideas and try them, McGovern embodied the essence of servant leadership. His influence in China, for example, was amplified by his consistent demonstration of respect and devotion to employees who had experienced nothing but state-controlled, central authoritarian leadership. Here was a powerful, rich American businessman who arrived just as China began to open its business borders and who actually listened and engaged with them and urged them to lead in their own style. They rewarded him by building *China Computerworld* into that country's most successful business publication, and IDG China grew into both a flourishing publishing empire and later a venture capital firm.

The Chinese IDG staff was in awe of this huge, gregarious American who defied all the stereotypes they had about capitalism and American aggressiveness. Karen Ren, an IDG vice president in China, often accompanied McGovern when he visited China. Each visit was a cultural experience, a chance to learn a bit more about the Chinese people, the IDG employees, the language, and the best way to succeed in this emerging global economy.

Starting in 2001, Ren became McGovern's personal assistant during many of his visits. She had spent her college years in the United States and spoke impeccable English. She was also a keen observer of business environments and the impact leaders have on employees. She kept notes on McGovern's many visits and the traits he exhibited on those visits.

Ren recounted how diligent McGovern was in paying attention to details. If he was going to attend an IDG-sponsored high-tech fair in Shenzhen, he would ask her for the numbers of expected attendees and booths that were sold, as well as the theme of the fair. He was prepared for all questions he would get from Chinese reporters at the event. With his photographic memory, he would remember every detail, from the names of family members of employees celebrating 10-year IDG anniversaries, to revenue and profit numbers for every Asian IDG publication when meeting with IDG unit managers at the Asia-Pacific managers meeting.

McGovern's affable and engaging nature helped him get along with everyone, from employees of the lowest rank to Chinese government officials. Ren pointed out that many foreigners are uncomfortable dealing with Chinese government officials because of the cautious nature of these encounters. McGovern, from his earliest forays into China, found ways to have the conversations and forge strong and rewarding relationships built upon mutual respect and trust.

Having set up shop in China so far ahead of the competition, McGovern was revered as a visionary business leader and often received VIP treatment. Hugo Shong noted that he accompanied McGovern on at least 110 of those 130 visits to China, serving as translator, guide, and business partner. He arranged for McGovern to meet with Chinese presidents Jiang Zemin and later Hu Jintao. Shong would always brief him prior to meetings, but it was McGovern's capacity for engaging these leaders that paid dividends. "He loved China," Shong said. "He was treated like a head of state. And he was really good at talking with the media. People loved him. He became like a spokesman for China's economy."

McGovern never tired of learning new things. He carried a small notebook wherever he went and constantly jotted reminders of things he learned or wanted to know. He repeatedly asked Ren to teach him Chinese words and phrases, and he made a point to learn a few new phrases on each visit. By the next visit, he spoke these phrases fluently in the proper context.

An admirer of Eastern philosophy and culture, McGovern quickly grasped the crucial intersection of business and social traditions. For Chinese businessmen, a meal is an important meeting opportunity, and the Chinese have a wide-ranging and eclectic taste for exotic dishes. McGovern would often be offered exotic local cuisine that most Americans would refuse. On one occasion in China, the host served donkey meat, a local delicacy, and Ren leaned over and explained what it was and that he needn't try it. But McGovern tried everything, and using chopsticks, he gobbled down the meat and complimented his host. Needless to say, his hosts were immensely impressed. Here was an American who knew how to eat.

Early IDG China employees, who light up when speaking about McGovern and the opportunities he gave them, recall that on a visit in 1982, he and Lore joined them in the lunchroom at the offices of *China Computerworld* and made dumplings, a dish

McGovern felt a deep connection to China, its people, and its culture.

he came to love. The idea that a rich American businessman like McGovern would go into the kitchen, roll up his sleeves, and learn to make Chinese dumplings left an indelible impression. This type of self-effacing humility was rare in successful business leaders. In China, it had a cumulative effect over the years, all to the good of IDG.

CHINESE VENTURE

With a population of 1.3 billion, a burgeoning economy, and a fast-growing middle class, China remains a controversial enigma, a communist regime operating in a global market economy. As all of today's top technology players—from Google to Facebook—have discovered, the landscape there is more than challenging, but it is a market most corporations covet as essential. Considering the current environment, it makes McGovern's achievements in China especially impressive. It required a classic loose-tight management style and an ability to navigate an obstacle course of government and business interests.

Jim Casella, a former IDG executive who ran *InfoWorld* and was later promoted to chief operating officer at IDG headquarters, got a rare chance to do business with McGovern after Casella left IDG to join Reed Elsevier, an international publishing house. Casella said he gained more insight into McGovern after he left IDG. He was surprised one day when he received an unexpected call from McGovern suggesting a publishing partnership in China.

"You have some great brands like *Variety*, and they've never been brought to China, or anywhere outside the U.S.," McGovern said. "They're growing and the demand for film in China is great." Casella agreed, and the result was a new joint venture that at its zenith produced 10 magazine titles, two research brands, and 175 new jobs in Beijing.

"I really got tremendous insight into how he operated," Casella said. "He liked that China was dynamic. He saw earlier than anybody else the potential growth. And he didn't have to compete with Bill Ziff there. He could go in and do what he wanted to do."

Others were intrigued by McGovern's success in China. Jim Breyer, a billionaire venture capitalist who today heads his own venture firm, Breyer Capital, is considered one of the world's savviest venture capitalists. His father, John Breyer, was among IDG's first employees, and the young Breyer was in grade school when he first met McGovern. McGovern made a point of trading baseball cards with the eight-year-old Red Sox fan, and in so doing, taught Breyer his very first lessons about business. Rather than letting his team loyalty determine which cards to hold and which to trade, McGovern counseled him on the importance of acquiring the cards of the best players such as Willie Mays or Hank Aaron. "You should rank the Red Sox players lower," McGovern told him. "Don't let your fondness for the Red Sox color your judgment." Optimize instead for Willie Mays, he suggested.

"The lesson he taught me about focusing on the very best is something I remember to this day," Breyer said.

In 2002, as managing partner for Accel Partners, Breyer wanted to learn more about the emerging Internet market in China and made a trip to see firsthand what was happening. Like McGovern, he had an intense cultural as well as investment interest in China. He met with Tencent and Baidu and other nascent Internet start-ups and talked to many entrepreneurs. He returned to Silicon Valley and convinced his partners that China was a market ripe for investment. All of Asia—including Singapore, Hong Kong, and Taipei—was rumbling with new ventures, but Breyer believed Beijing was the place to be. Partnering with a firm already in place in China would be the best path forward. Due to its prominent position, IDG Capital was clearly the preferred partner. IDG had more than a decade head start in China's venture community. Its first-mover status gave it an advantageous foothold for anyone fortunate enough to become a partner.

In 2004, as chairman of the National Venture Capital Association in the United States, Breyer met with Hugo Shong, who was his Chinese counterpart as chairman of the China Venture Capital Association. They discussed potential opportunities for Accel Partners in China. The meeting confirmed for Breyer that a partnership with IDG Capital would be the most desirable investment path.

Not surprising, the top venture firms like Sequoia, Kleiner Perkins, Oak Investment Partners, and others were moving aggressively into this fertile market, and they all were eyeing possible partnerships with IDG. Breyer called McGovern and began the conversation about a possible partnership. In this new flourishing environment, McGovern was more open to a partnership than he had been in the past. Breyer made three trips to China and several to Boston to meet with McGovern and Shong about moving forward. By 2005, things were heating up.

Due to their family connections, McGovern had a special fondness for Breyer and had been more than impressed that his young protégé had emerged as a hugely successful businessman. Baseball card wisdom had clearly paid off. But he also had to consider the best options for IDG, and he took seriously the offers being put on the table by the top-tier firms.

"He welcomed me," Breyer recalled. "He was very gracious and warm, and he said, 'We have a number of options, but Jim, if you can put something meaningful together, I would love to work with you.'"

A series of negotiations followed with IDG Capital, and Shong and McGovern were clear about their requirements. In May 2005, Breyer and McGovern shook hands and agreed to move forward together with a joint venture between Accel Partners and IDG Capital Partners in Beijing. "It came to my attention later that a couple of the other firms, when they heard about Pat's decision, went directly to Pat with terms that may have been better and significantly higher in terms of the economics for IDG," Breyer recalled. "But I knew once somebody shakes Pat McGovern's hand, he was a great partner, and that's how we always did business going forward."

Breyer knew that family history had played a part in McGovern's decision, but their shared passion for China, Chinese culture, and the long-term nature of the venture capital business in China all played a big role. "He was an extraordinary leader and businessman," Breyer said. "We were together in China about a dozen times, and it was always intellectually and personally invigorating."

For Breyer, the spring of 2005 turned out to be the seminal stretch of his career. In April, he made one of the first significant venture investments in Mark Zuckerberg's Facebook start-up and joined the Facebook board. A month later, he signed the deal with IDG Capital. It's difficult to remember, but in 2005, Facebook was just 15 months removed from the Harvard dorm room where it had been born, was still known as thefacebook.com, and had just three million users at 800 colleges. The bet Breyer made was hardly a sure thing, but it turned out to be monumental.

"A dozen years later, I look back at how fundamental those months were," Breyer said. "A lot of people then didn't think the

Internet would come back after it had crashed, so both these invest-ments were contrarian moves. I love contrarian investment moves."

OUTSIDE CHINA

Though he came to India later in his career, McGovern brought a similar level of curiosity and enthusiasm to the venture capital firm he funded in Bangalore. T. C. Meenakshisundaram, known as TCM, was one of the cofounders of IDG Ventures India. He first met McGovern in 2006. He was astonished at McGovern's stamina and determination on these visits, some of which entailed eight meetings a day for five straight days with up to 40 companies and young entrepreneurs. Despite his inevitable optimism and genuine interest in every entrepreneur he met, McGovern, as a member of the firm's investment committee, didn't hesitate to push back if he thought badly of a prospective investment.

"In a few cases, he said, 'Don't do this,'" TCM recalled. "For example, we were looking very enthusiastically at an electric vehi-cle company, and he said that the complexities associated with this, while it might be an interesting business, it was not a VC-fundable business. It has high capital requirements and there is no tech-nology leverage. In the long run, it's still an automobile company which will consume a lot of capital."

According to TCM, McGovern was never demanding or insistent. He simply made clear his logic and believed that his cred-ibility ought to speak for itself. "We were strongly recommending an investment in this venture," TCM said. "He never said, 'It's my money, so no.' He allowed us time to get back to him if we had more information. What we found was that his instincts were right."

McGovern also prodded IDG Ventures India to diversify and not rely on IDG to fully fund its offerings. He was more than will-ing to provide 100 percent of the capital for the first fund, but after that, he insisted they find other limited partners to take 50 percent of the second fund. With the third IDG fund, he reduced his investment to 25 percent.

"He wanted to help us build our track record at the beginning and then start diversifying the limited partner base. His vision has played out," said TCM.

PAT MATH

One of McGovern's favored business tactics was using his mastery of the numbers to push IDG toward unremitting growth. He believed that when you, as a business unit leader, have mastered your numbers, you will no longer be reading *numbers* any more than you read words when reading a book. You will be reading *meanings*.

His ability to forecast success in untapped markets was based on inhaling data, mostly from his own IDC researchers, but also from countless outside resources. When he traveled, he toted one suitcase for his clothes and another, even larger bag for books, magazines, and reports. His son-in-law, Edward Jackson, recalled helping him as he packed for a rugged trip to the South Pole to officially launch *Computerworld Antarctica*, which would signify that IDG did business on all seven of the world's continents. McGovern realized he needed to cut way back on his luggage, and he preferred to jettison vital warm clothing in favor of his reading material.

To many of his managers, McGovern's insistence on stretch budgets was known as "Pat Math," and it entailed a prescribed back-and-forth in regular managers meetings. McGovern would hear what a unit leader had laid out for the coming year or more, and then he would gently but firmly reset the numbers, usually significantly higher.

In meetings, he could sit for hours, literally, and grill a business unit manager on the numbers, chiding that executive to reach and stretch further, even when it seemed impossible. If the pushback was too intense, McGovern's face would turn red and he would get

McGovern at the South Pole for the launch of *Computerworld Antarctica.*

quiet, which was a signal that he was not pleased with the conversation. But he never yelled or shut anyone down.

His patience was legendary. "He was a master at not pulling the plug, not giving up on something too soon," said Bill Sell, a former IDG executive. Unlike publicly traded companies, where one or two down quarters would dictate some punitive measure, McGovern would see through the business downturns.

In fact, IDC, the company's original research business, had struggled for two decades to turn a profit. "Pat didn't close it down," said IDC's CEO Kirk Campbell. "He believed in it." Despite notable resentment from other business units at carrying IDC along, McGovern refused to give up on the unit, which had just $30 million in revenues in 1990 when Campbell took over. By the mid-1990s, IDC began to turn things around, and by 2018, grew into a $360 million business with 1,900 employees in 50 countries.

ENGLAND SWINGS

When Kit Gould joined IDG's UK operations in 1996, he found himself in a business unit that had yet to please McGovern. IDG publications had never achieved the level of success in the UK market that one might have expected. McGovern thought the United Kingdom was the toughest media market in the world, and yet he was determined to make a go of it. Gould joined IDG from a competitor, so he knew the market intimately and felt he could bring something bold to the table. He was also familiar with McGovern and his reputation. "It had always been a thorn in Pat's side that the U.K. had never been very successful for IDG," Gould recalled.

Gould would hold several positions within IDG on both the media and venture capital sides before becoming CEO and managing director for IDG Communications in the United Kingdom and Sweden. His first meeting with McGovern set the tone for his next two decades with IDG.

IDG had acquired a British publication called *PC Advisor* as yet another attempt to get into the UK market. Gould was brought on board to shepherd the publication. He started on a Monday morning and discovered he was due to be in Morocco on Wednesday for a product line meeting. He jumped on a plane to Marrakesh where he met Pat Kenealy, who was then CEO of *PCWorld*. Kenealy greeted Gould and asked him if he was ready for his first meeting with McGovern the following week. This was news to Gould, who asked if there was an agenda. "Yes," Kenealy responded. "That's where you present your five-year plan."

Fighting off panic, Gould raced to piece together a plan in a matter of days. Kenealy peppered him with questions he knew McGovern would ask. For example: "If you increase the cover price by 10 percent, how many more issues would you sell?" Gould replied, "I don't know," and Kenealy said, "Yes, I know, but you're more likely to make a better guess than me or Pat." He worked through the social hours during the Morocco meeting, returned to London on Friday, and put together a budget for the next five years, which he got printed at Kinko's on Monday afternoon. On Tuesday morning, feeling utterly unprepared, he sat down with McGovern.

Unbeknownst to Gould, McGovern was under the impression that after the purchase price for *PC Advisor*, he wouldn't need to invest more than $60,000 to get the publication spruced up and ready for a relaunch. Gould had never heard this lowball figure, and in his business plan, he had included improvements costing in excess of seven figures, mostly for quality staff, to bring his blueprint to fruition. When he heard McGovern mention $60,000, he assumed his career at IDG would be short-lived.

Instead, McGovern quietly listened to Gould's presentation, asked sensible questions, and Gould came away with a revelation. "His questions were designed to test whether you knew what you were talking about," he explained. "It wasn't whether you were right or wrong, but whether you've thought through everything to arrive at that number."

With a veteran's savvy, McGovern suggested modifications, asked whether a target goal was reasonable, and avoided dictating or demanding a specific result. They agreed on a two-and-a-half-year time frame to turn a profit, which Gould accomplished in 18 months. And he learned quickly that once a unit manager delivered what McGovern wanted, whether to turn a profit or achieve market leadership, he rarely said no to any future plans.

"Quite often, during conversations with him, he asked questions to get you thinking," Gould said. "He didn't really care about the answer or the outcome. He cared about how you were thinking about it. That's the impression I got."

Over time, as a degree of trust was established from producing desired results and exceeding expectations, McGovern would back off and give way to individual leadership. Gould recalled sitting in meetings and seeing new, younger managers come in and go through a similar initiation. It left an indelible mark, very much for the good, Gould said.

Like others in IDG's long history, Gould would see McGovern in his glory during the quarterly managers meetings in which each country manager had 60 to 90 minutes to present a progress report. McGovern was ready for every presentation.

"The preparation he would do on your detail was astounding," Gould said. "He had notes and reports, and you'd think, 'Holy crap, he's got all those notes. I hope I've got answers' when he fires questions." Gould learned to spend a couple of days in preparation before each meeting, anticipating the most difficult questions he could be asked so he would have answers at the ready. Such attention to detail stuck with Gould through his career. "I know how to prepare for meetings now," he said, laughing.

Working with McGovern in this loose-tight environment provided an indelible lesson in management for Gould. Among the lessons he took away:

- Get what you need in place and worry about making money further down the road. Look at the long term.

- Invest in the quality of the product, especially the quality of the editorial output.

- Find a natural optimism and be supportive when people start a new project or venture. They don't always get it right the first time, and it might take a little longer than anticipated.

- Recruit the very best people you can. Listen, argue, discuss, and agree on a plan and fund them, perhaps a bit more than they need to help generate growth and innovation. Then get the hell out of the way.

Gould learned that McGovern believed if people come to feel that the business they are running is theirs, they will perform that much better. This sense of ownership was not simply words but deeds. If a country leader made his or her financial metrics, "you could do anything you wanted," Gould said. "Very few companies allowed you to set prices, set the positioning, set the targets, write a plan, recruit the resources you need. This was a different way to do things."

At its zenith, the sun never set on the IDG empire. McGovern had successfully planted flags in every market, both major and minor, around the globe. Part of IDG's success in this demanding global march was that McGovern created a "family" of country managers and brought them together for worldwide meetings on a regular basis. It was a support group without borders, and rather than business units competing against each other, the only vested interest was in making IDG a success. A sense of camaraderie coursed throughout the company. Gould would encounter somebody at the meeting who would say, "We're thinking of launching a business in Spain, and I'd immediately say, 'Well, you want to speak to Manuel, and here's his number.'"

In fact, there was an unspoken rule among country leaders that if somebody asked for help for a trusted colleague, "you always took the meeting," no questions asked. "That was enormously powerful in and around Europe," Gould declared. To be able to connect country leaders together and with prospective new ventures at any time "gave you an international view that none of your competitors had.

"When I first joined IDG, I remember being quite taken aback at just how supportive all my colleagues were," Gould added. "They didn't know me. I hadn't been there. But within three or four meetings with them, I honestly can say they became lifelong friends."

Perhaps the most inspirational takeaway was the simplest. "Pat really believed that people are fundamentally good," Gould said. "And if you give people a task and the resources and support them well enough, 90 percent of the time they'll deliver what you want. Maybe even impress you by doing more." That feeling, which was rare in most corporate settings, had a bonus outcome: "It made you want to be as good as you could possibly be," Gould said.

TAKEAWAYS

▶▶ Make curiosity a driving business advantage—but never forget that someone has to have the final word.

▶▶ Practice servant leadership.

▶▶ Never stop learning. Always remain curious.

▶▶ When you master your numbers, you will no longer be reading numbers, you will be reading *meanings*.

▶▶ Pepper your people with questions, not to get specific answers but to get them thinking about bigger questions.

10

LESSON NINE
Chief Encouragement Officer: Never Stop Cheering Them On

Our chief want is someone who will inspire
us to be what we know we could be.
—RALPH WALDO EMERSON

For a man who flew an average of 300,000 miles a year or more for much of his long career, Patrick McGovern had an unexpected phobia: he was afraid of flying. Specifically, he hated flying on small planes. Yet one day in 1998, he called his son Patrick III and said, "Hey, what are you doing this afternoon?"

"Nothing," his son replied. "Why?"

"Do you want to pick me up and go for a ride?" McGovern asked cryptically. Perplexed but curious, his son, an entrepreneur and technology investor, agreed and picked him up at his Hillsborough, California, home. They drove two hours and arrived at a small airstrip. "What are we doing here?" the younger McGovern asked.

"Just you wait," his father replied. And soon it became clear; this very large man with his fear of small airplanes was going to try skydiving. "He really hated small planes, but he decided, 'I'm going to do this thing,'" his son recalled.

After 15 minutes of instruction, McGovern climbed aboard the diminutive skydiving plane with the instructor who would jump in tandem with him. The plane took off, circled the area up to 10,000 feet, and from the ground, the younger McGovern watched in awe as his father leaped from the plane.

On the way to the ground, strapped to his tandem partner, McGovern held aloft a homemade sign for a videographer who accompanied the jumpers. "IDG Is Number One!" the sign read. And as he landed, with the video camera rolling, he began to yell, "I see Bob! I see Walter! I see Ted!" referring to various IDG executives who were going to be attending that year's worldwide managers meeting. "Now that's the way you do it! Don't just sit there, take charge! Don't look at the single trees, look at the whole forest! Go, IDG! You can do it!"

The skydive, it turned out, was an integral part of McGovern's presentation at the upcoming meeting. On stage after his skydive, McGovern kicked off the festivities by addressing the group of leaders. "Everyone here knows that I can do just about everything, but Walter, what's my big hang-up?" he called out to Walter Boyd.

"Well, you don't like small planes," Boyd responded. And then, "Ted, what do you think?" McGovern asked. "That's it. You don't like small planes," echoed Ted Bloom. At that point, the room darkened, and McGovern cued the video of him jumping out of the plane and unfurling his IDG sign with his inspiring message for his managers. The room erupted. They knew McGovern liked to push the envelope, try new things, and stir the pot. But this was over the top—what kind of CEO jumps out of airplanes in order to create an inspirational video?—and it reinforced for IDG leaders that he truly would do anything to motivate the troops.

McGovern often referred to himself as the CEO (chief encouragement officer) whose main role was to offer support and

JUMP INTO IT . . . MAKE IT HAPPEN THE IDG WAY!

Best Regards, Pat McGovern

McGovern would leap from a plane to cheer on the company.

inspiration to his employees. In a 1983 front-page profile in the *Wall Street Journal*, McGovern was described as a "relentless cheerleader" who "sends reporters and editors a stream of congratulatory notes, usually full of exclamation marks, on stationery that has a rainbow design at the top and the headline: "Good News!""[1]

This was fundamental to McGovern's leadership, and he never wavered, over 50 years, in keeping it central to his management philosophy. The truest path to organizational success is with an engaged, motivated, and talented pool of employees who believe in the mission because they have embraced it as their own. Constant and visible encouragement and support were the means McGovern employed to achieve this goal, and it worked by any measure.

Robert Mahoney, the president of the Belmont Savings Bank in Belmont, Massachusetts, and a member of IDG's board, was struck by McGovern's essential benevolence in his management style. "Kind and smart don't usually go hand in hand," Mahoney said. "Jack Welch was smart, but he was never accused of being kind. You can live with problems, but having people feel good about themselves and not weighed down by criticism is a powerful way to manage. It was not for show with Pat. He was just that way."

For Mahoney, spending time with McGovern was a master class in leadership. "He gave me a sense that you can lead and be strong without being mean; that you can give people hope without creating an IOU; that you can draw a picture of what the future would look like if everyone pulled together on the same oar and make that a very exciting oar to grab onto."

Nearly every one of the tens of thousands of employees who worked for the company has personal McGovern stories. McGovern traveled around the globe not only as IDG's chairman and CEO but as its goodwill ambassador. His Good News notes always included a personal comment extolling the high-quality work and its impact on IDG. It was difficult to find an office or cubicle without one or two of these memos tacked to an employee's bulletin board. They were simple notes but treasured by the people who received them. In most corporations, where the gulf between the CEO and the workers is an impassable chasm, this kind of personal connection was rare.

"It'll sound like a stupid cliché," said George Colony, founder and chairman of Forrester Research, a technology research firm and IDC rival, "but nice guys can finish first here. In a world where every CEO is trying to get as much compensation as possible and [is] so self-centered, he felt like one of the last magnanimous, decent, and straight-shooting people. Obviously, that is very connected to his success."

Colony was always impressed, when he met with McGovern, by how generous McGovern was to a competitor. He openly offered sage advice, wished Colony good luck, and seemed genuinely welcoming in an industry known more for its ferocious competitiveness. It was this quality in McGovern that kept so many employees on board for so long. "I know many of the people at IDC, and many of them stayed with compensation which was 20 percent or 30 percent below the industry average because they

TO: Patrick Kenney   cc: David Hill

FROM: Patrick McGovern

DATE: October 28, 2008

Dear Patrick:

Congratulations to you and your associate Don Botts on doing an excellent job in building the database to allow Peter Longo's syndication group to have a very valuable service to sell!

You were able to continue to enhance the effectiveness of the service on short notice, resulting in a very positive marketplace reaction to this service!

Well done!

Best regards,

A Good News memo.

believed in him and they wanted to be near him. He had that magnetism because of his decency."

McGovern practiced the same kind of enthusiastic hands-on support at the McGovern Institute for Brain Research (MIBR) at MIT. Most donors whose names are etched in the marble facades of academic buildings have written large checks, cut a ribbon, and visited once or twice a year for photo opportunities. McGovern was a regular presence at the MIBR, and he did a deep dive into the work being done there. He personally encouraged the staff to build a world-class research environment, and he was genuinely passionate about this work. But he also recognized the value of serving as an organization's loudest cheerleader. In fact, he sent the same Good News notes to MIBR researchers when he learned of an award received, a research breakthrough achieved, or the publication of an important paper. "He was always giving people praise when something good happened," said Bob Desimone, the director of the MIBR.

For Jeffrey Rayport, a Harvard Business School professor and IDG board member, the notes were a reminder of how potent a simple gesture can be. "There's nobody I've ever met at IDG who didn't, in an unprompted moment, bring up the power and importance of those words of encouragement from him," Rayport said.

AN INCREDIBLE EFFECT

Given the empire he built, the scope of IDG's influence, and the milestones across 50 years of leadership, it is remarkable how a single gesture McGovern practiced year after year resonated. His holiday visits to employees to hand out bonus checks and share a few moments of personal encouragement made a deep and lasting impression. If you speak to any random group of IDG employees, past or present, nearly everyone will have a similar story to recount of the Christmas bonus visits, his personal comments, his remarkable memory about past encounters, and his willingness to travel around the country for weeks at holiday time to personally thank everyone, from the top executives to the maintenance staff, for their contributions to IDG's success.

Speaking to the *Wall Street Journal* in 1983, Stewart Alsop, the former editor of *InfoWorld* and a well-known industry pundit, recalled McGovern's visit. "The first Christmas I was at *InfoWorld*, he stopped to talk to one of the junior copy editors," Alsop said. "He remembered precisely what they talked about the year before. The copy editor was absolutely stunned. That has an incredible effect on people here."[2]

The effort McGovern put in to celebrate the holidays with his employees was nothing short of monumental. It began in the company's earliest days, McGovern recalled, and simply caught on. "We had 14 employees then, and I thought I'd write out some holiday cards," he said. "We only had two rooms, so I walked around and handed them out. And fortunately, that started a tradition."

Most CEOs would scoff at the time and effort it required and label it a waste of important executive time. Not only did McGovern spend two weeks or more in December traveling around the United States to visit every IDG office and meet every employee, but he signed every holiday card—sometimes as many as 5,000—into which the bonus was inserted. Mary Dolaher, his executive assistant, was always astounded (and exhausted) by the effort.

"We worked a lot of hours during the Christmas season," Dolaher said. "He would insist on signing every card. One year I said, 'I can sign them better than you,' but he wouldn't let me. We sat there until four in the morning while I stuffed cash in the envelopes." McGovern would go back to his Boston hotel suite for a few hours of sleep and be right back at his desk early the next morning.

Dolaher relished working with McGovern and knowing that she had exceeded even his grand expectations. She took on more and more of his cheerleading activities, including identifying recipients for the Good News notes. She would talk to managers around the world for recommendations and scour IDG publications for stories that looked important, seeking worthy recipients of one of the 15 to 20 notes he would send each week.

"I would think to myself, 'I'm 28. Why am I so tired?'" Dolaher recalled. "It was impossible to keep up with him. My favorite sound was when I'd hear him take his jacket off the back of the office door. 'Oh, thank God, he's done.'"

Maggie Murphy, who succeeded Dolaher and worked as McGovern's assistant for 21 years, had a similar experience. "We would start the day after Thanksgiving, to my chagrin," said Murphy. "We never got a day off. I would ask him if he was sure he wanted to do all this again each year, and he'd say, 'Oh yeah, we have to do that.' "

If the bonus distribution wasn't enough, McGovern also hosted a lavish annual black-tie holiday party in a posh downtown Boston hotel. Dolaher and later Murphy had to coordinate that effort, for which no expense was spared, and every area employee was invited, along with a significant other, for an evening of food, drink, dancing, and expensive door prizes.

The highlight of the evening was the video presentations, which included candid photographs of employees at work, and a lengthy skit featuring McGovern and the IDG executive team portraying the *Star Trek* crew or a Beatles-like rock band or some other costume comedy. Well before the proliferation of the Internet, smartphones, Facebook, and YouTube, everyone got a charge out of seeing their image on a big screen at the celebration.

Kelly Conlin, a former IDG CEO, remembers the annual trek to a local production studio where the four or five top executives would get into costume and "display what bad actors we were." The "scripts" were written by a few "down and out journalist friends" whom Conlin contracted. One of them, Conlin pointed out, went on to become a successful television writer with credits on *Frasier* and *Desperate Housewives*. "He went from writing IDG scripts to Hollywood royalty," Conlin laughed.

In fact, the acting was so bad that it was funny, and the ultimate message of each video was little more than a thinly disguised IDG cheerleading opportunity for McGovern. Corny as these were, McGovern ended each by booming out his signature "The best is yet to come!" admonition, and the crowd always cheered loudly. In an era of skyrocketing CEO compensation and the ever-widening gulf between top management and workers, McGovern's commitment to a personal connection with his employees was a welcome

McGovern as *Star Trek*'s Captain Kirk with Walter Boyd as Spock in a holiday party skit.

anachronism. Even though much of the IDG staff was young, they were seasoned enough to realize that this kind of enthusiasm, access, and commitment from the top person was unique.

When Chris Shipley, who ran IDG's popular DEMO conference for many years, was given a company lifetime achievement award at her last event, McGovern presented the trophy. At DEMO, a catchy dance tune was played to open the show and in between presentations. Shipley, touched by the award, laughed when McGovern said, "I wish we could do that dance." "We can," Shipley replied. She demonstrated the dance steps, and soon, the two were sashaying back and forth across the stage, to the delight of the crowd. "He had his finger on the pulse of the company," Shipley said, "but he was also a person who could put aside any pretension and dance in front of 800 business leaders. He did what it took to be connected, and his authenticity was what I remember the most about him."

McGovern was indeed authentic, but he had an ulterior motive. Retaining quality employees was not easy, and replacing them was time-consuming and costly. His investment in keeping everyone happy and enthusiastic paid off many times over.

"Sometimes I talk to executive recruiters, and they say, 'It's hard to hire anyone from IDG because they all feel they have a personal relationship with you,'" McGovern said. "'They say the chairman comes by, knows my name, knows what I do and why it's important, how many children I have, and he always tells me if there's any way I can help you, just call me directly.' What's amazing is no one ever calls. But psychologically, it builds a family spirit."

McGovern believed deeply that everybody has moments of insecurity in their lives and careers. So an encouraging note from the CEO, reminding them that they are doing a good job, is a powerful tool for fending off executive recruiters. "If some recruiter is calling them, they say, 'No, I'm very happy here,'" he added.

For an introvert, McGovern grew to love the spotlight and used every opportunity to forge a motivational event to stir up the troops. He didn't have the bully pulpit presence of a Tony Robbins, but he connected on a deeper level. Devotion and consistency forged an unassailable image in IDG employees' minds that the man in the dark suit truly cared about them.

In 1987, when *Computerworld* celebrated its twentieth anniversary, McGovern asked Dolaher to find a high school marching band to parade from IDG's headquarters on Speen Street in Framingham to *Computerworld*'s offices several blocks away. Dolaher conscripted the Westwood High School marching band and outfitted them with a huge *Computerworld* birthday greeting. Dressed in a full Sgt. Pepper–like drum major uniform ("It was 20 years ago today . . ."), McGovern led the parade while he waved his baton, and he and Dolaher, dressed as lead majorette, steered the band onto *Computerworld*'s back patio. Veteran employees cheered. Newer employees watched with mouths agape, astonished that the CEO of the massive company would display this kind of enthusiasm.

McGovern leading a marching band on *Computerworld*'s twentieth anniversary.

McGovern always walked a fine line of formality with most people, being unfailingly polite but often a bit stiff and reserved. This could and did change dramatically when the occasion called for it. He could, it turned out, party with the best of them. On the many worldwide managers meetings, it was McGovern who kept the hotel bar open, downing drinks and turning business into pleasure. He loved to get the party started, and he had a remarkable capacity to hold his liquor. He could down seven or eight beers and regularly drank his employees under the table. "He was playful and fun, and he wanted people to see him as one of them," Dolaher said. "He wanted contributors, not distractors, and if people enjoyed what they were doing, they would work harder."

When Eckhard Utpadel, IDG Germany's onetime country manager, accompanied McGovern to Prague to set up a Czech *Computerworld*, they couldn't get a flight back to Munich, so Utpadel rented a car and they drove back through a snowstorm over the mountains. It was a harrowing four-hour drive, and the pair arrived in Munich after midnight. Utpadel explained to McGovern that it was Fasching or Carnival time in Munich, a city-wide party that included masquerading hordes, heavy drinking,

and parades through the street. After an exhausting day of meetings and a long drive, McGovern insisted on going out to enjoy the
carnival. "Do you have a costume for me?" he implored Utpadel.
They partied until 4 a.m. "That was Pat. He was really amazing,"
Utpadel said.

"He was sober and straitlaced," added Walter Boyd, "but when
he cut loose, there was nobody quite like him. He went wild. Traveling with him was an experience."

The stories grew into legends. Even the disasters burnished the
company's image. In the 1970s, for example, when IDG invested
in the Computer Caravan, a traveling trade show that would set up
in 10 cities in 10 weeks, McGovern decided to extend the concept
to Europe. The first event was to be held at the lavish Georges V
Hotel, a Paris landmark. The trade show was set up in the grand
ballroom, and IDG had hired a young event planner to spice
things up.

McGovern suggested bringing in a camel to symbolize the caravan concept, an idea he had used to hype the event back in the
United States but one fraught with potential disaster. The event
planner went ahead anyway and arranged to have a handler bring a
camel into the Georges V ballroom. All went according to plan until
the dromedary decided to help itself to huge trays of hors d'oeuvres
being offered to the guests by waiters circulating around the room.
Emboldened, the camel began to parade around the ballroom, while
its frantic trainer tried in vain to get it under control. It headed out of
the ballroom into the hotel's posh lobby, dropping massive piles of
camel dung on the expensive oriental rugs, while McGovern howled
in laughter. Sometimes you win, sometimes you lose, McGovern
figured, but it was well worth it if it was fun and memorable.

EMPLOYEES FIRST

Many management books have been written over the decades
about ways to win friends and influence business. McGovern's

dedication to his employees' well-being has always been cited as a key cornerstone of IDG's success. Such behavior could not guarantee increased sales and profits, but the net effect was just that.

In the world of business, where massive egos banged up against each other, McGovern had a way of creating strong attachments with his managers around the globe. When Axel Leblois, the French executive who served as CEO of IDG Communications for a short but dramatic period, was recruited to run Honeywell Bull in France, it was an offer he couldn't refuse. But his departure was an emotional one.

"We had a very tight bond," Leblois recalled. "It was a strong intellectual and emotional bond. That was the nature of his leadership. He was not an impersonal manager. He knew about you, cared about you, and it was more than just a regular management relationship."

Paul Gillin, a former editor in chief of *Computerworld*, also spent time working for IDG's main competitor, Ziff Davis. His time there was a dramatic counterpoint to his IDG experience, especially McGovern's affable availability.

"Ziff was the opposite of IDG's culture," Gillin said. "It was a classic New York business: extremely political, lots of backbiting, very little loyalty, a lot of infighting. Mostly, there was no Uncle Bill Ziff coming around to shake employees' hands and deliver a holiday bonus. You really didn't see him."

Gillin was especially taken by another McGovern tradition, a dinner out with the boss on an employee's tenth anniversary with the company. "We met at the Four Seasons in Boston," Gillin recalled. "The dinner lasted three hours. He was so generous with his time. Here was the head of this global company with thousands of employees, and he took that kind of time to celebrate an individual employee."

Maryfran Johnson, IDG executive director of CIO programs and *Computerworld*'s first woman editor in chief, recalled arriving at the Ritz Hotel in downtown Boston on a frigid April night in 2000 for her tenth anniversary dinner. She was frantic because the traffic had made her late. But when she arrived, McGovern stood outside, smiling broadly and holding a big bouquet of flowers for her. Rather than being annoyed, he pulled a disposable camera from his pocket and asked the doorman to take their picture for the IDG World Update company newsletter. Then he "whisked me through the revolving doors into the Ritz's magnificent dining room, where chilled champagne awaited," she remembered. "This was one of the most memorable, delightful meals of my life."

For Johnson, McGovern had what she described as "a phenomenally high emotional quotient (EQ). He really connected with people," she said. "When he was talking to you, you were the only person in the world."

Murphy, McGovern's longtime assistant, noted how much time and effort McGovern put into these dinners. When the company was smaller, most of the dinners were one-on-one with the employee. As IDG grew and the numbers required group dinners, McGovern never stopped insisting on having Murphy compile notable facts about each celebrant: their background, their families, their hobbies, where they went to school. "He wanted something to make that person feel comfortable about themselves," Murphy said. "He told me, 'I know you've planned hundreds of these for me, but for that person, it is their first and only time.' His respect for the employee was so important."

Robert Farmer, a legendary Democratic fund-raiser and close personal friend of McGovern, recalled being invited along to a 10-year anniversary dinner for two Japanese employees at IDG in Tokyo. "We went to a very nice Japanese restaurant, and Pat made the appropriate toasts to the two women," said Farmer. "It was all terrific. When we finished the meal and went outside, it was pouring rain. Fortunately, there were two limos out front, which Pat had arranged. To my chagrin, the two employees each got into one of the limos, leaving us to get drenched while running to find a taxi. That was Pat, always putting the employees first."

Indeed, not satisfied with the anniversary dinner concept, McGovern added a 20-year anniversary reward: a trip for two anywhere in the world. These perks paid dividends in a corporate culture that felt so familial and welcoming. But it was IDG's innovative employee stock option plan or ESOP that left the most indelible mark on people's lives.

THE ESOP

McGovern always believed that his employees should share in the company's success. Though he always retained a majority ownership of IDG, in the 1970s, he instituted a profit-sharing plan that was a forerunner to the ESOP, which debuted in 1987 when President Reagan shepherded a massive tax reform bill through Congress. New regulations allowed for the establishment of a formal ESOP without tax penalties. For early and long-term IDG employees, the ESOP, which contributed the equivalent of a percentage of an employee's annual salary into an IDG stock fund, provided a startlingly potent retirement plan well before the advent of the 401(k). Because it was privately held, IDG's shares were valued each year by Marshall & Stevens, an independent appraisal firm, and during the go-go seventies and eighties, these shares soared in value. In time, a significant number of IDG veterans had accounts worth more than a million dollars, while many others accumulated six-figure retirement funds that they never would have garnered at most other companies.

In those heady days, McGovern would regularly tell gatherings of employees that his goal was to eventually have more than half the company's shares owned by the employees. He also promised that when IDG reached $1 billion in sales, he would take the company public. In that case, these accumulated shares promised to make hundreds if not thousands of employees wealthy. By the mid-1980s, well before the Silicon Valley IPO boom that created thousands of millionaires among the rank and file, IDG employees in the United States spent more than a little time fantasizing about their impending riches. In a 1996 interview with *Bloomberg*

Business News, McGovern went so far as to predict a public offering in 1998. He noted that employee stock ownership was growing 2 to 3 percent per year, and by the year 2000, "over half the company will be owned by employees."[3]

Whatever his intentions, the IPO for all of IDG never happened, though McGovern did approve the public offering for IDG Books in the late 1990s. In truth, McGovern always had trepidations about turning IDG into a public company. Ted Bloom, the company's president and chief financial officer, believed that McGovern didn't want the restrictions and headaches associated with a public company. Bloom couldn't imagine McGovern capitulating to a board that told him where he could and couldn't start new publications and invest in new ventures. Quarterly earnings pressure would have been the antithesis of McGovern's "Let's try it" leadership philosophy. "I don't think it ever was his desire to go public or he would have done it," Bloom said.

Some employees grumbled, despite accumulating hefty ESOP accounts. Others appreciated what they perceived as enormous generosity on McGovern's part for instituting such a plan. After a massive run-up in IDG's valuation, the ESOP lost nearly half its value when the dot-com bubble burst in 2001 and advertisers started pulling their ads from IDG publications. At some point, the ESOP was quietly replaced by a standard 401(k) retirement plan. But for thousands of US-based employees, the ESOP provided comfortable nest eggs that forever endeared McGovern and IDG to them.

Indeed, the impact of McGovern's largesse was tangible, and it was reflected at every level of the company, including with the board of directors. Rayport recalled how McGovern's unfailing encouragement during the 2008 economic crisis was crucial to IDG's survival. "These were close to existential issues, something close to a cash crisis," Rayport recalled. "It was quite remarkable, the power of Pat's optimism, his unfailing faith in the enterprise to make it through, a determination that there were going to be no wrong answers." Rayport said the board members gained a greater appreciation, during the crisis, of McGovern's ability to project a sense of stability, that all will be well, that IDG was on an important mission and it would get done. "It was a very impressive thing to see," Rayport said.

Even employees who left IDG under less than ideal circumstances were influenced by McGovern. John Battelle, chairman of the ill-fated *Industry Standard*, a once high-flying Internet business magazine acquired by IDG that crashed in 2001 in a highly visible flameout, told a *Boston Globe* reporter, "At heart, Pat is a familial figure. He loves his company. He is not a fist-pounding organization man. He is not a temperamental visionary like Jobs. He is not a hands-on manager like Jack Welch. He is his own character."[4]

To illustrate the point, Robert X. Cringely, a noted technology columnist for *InfoWorld* from 1987 to 1995, wrote a tribute to McGovern on his blog when McGovern died in 2014.

"When I was fired 18 years ago by *InfoWorld*, Pat knew about it," Cringely wrote. "It was a big enough deal that someone told him, and he didn't stop it because he trusted his executives to do the right thing. But when it became clear after months of rancor and hundreds of thousands in legal bills that it hadn't been the right thing, Pat and I met in a hotel suite in New York, handwrote an agreement, and he offered me back my old job. Understand this was my boss's, boss's, boss's boss asking me to return. I couldn't do it, but we stayed in touch. He always took my calls and answered my e-mail. And when he did, he always threw in three or four sentences to show that he had been reading or watching my work.

"There is something important in this about how people can work together, something I hope you find today in your organization. I never worked *for* Pat McGovern. I was always down in the engine room, shoveling words. But Pat knew about the engine room, understood its importance, and realized that the people down there *were* people and he ought to try to know them. The result was great loyalty, a better product, and a sense of literal ownership in the company that I retain today almost two decades later."[5]

Walter Boyd, who served as McGovern's right-hand man for decades, saw the evolution of an intrinsically shy and introverted man into the visible face and soul of the company. Boyd recalled how difficult it was for McGovern to go to an industry trade show and glad-hand a thousand people in three days. "It was never easy for him to do that, but he became an absolute master at it," Boyd said.

Boyd marveled at McGovern's photographic memory and how he used it to make instant connections with his employees. "His secretary sent him pages and pages of material on people in the company: what they were doing, what they had done, knowing he would likely meet them in the future," Boyd said. "Once he read it, it was there. If it had been in writing, he could quote a memo you wrote to him 20 years ago."

Though genuine, McGovern's deeds were not without calculation. "Pat was very aware of how everybody regarded him," Boyd said. "He cared a lot about that, and he worked very hard at it. His whole aim was to be the cheerleader. He loved that role, and he did it superbly. He made a point of being with people a great deal, and it wasn't always appreciated."

IDG's sales force, for example, had trepidations about a McGovern visit. If salespeople went a whole quarter without meeting their sales quota, they got a visit from McGovern, who would accompany them for a week's worth of sales calls, often filling entire days with back-to-back customer meetings. McGovern also fired off memos that weren't in the Good News category—tense and pointed notes that left no doubt he was displeased and expected answers. But those were rare in the greater scheme of his output.

Instead, McGovern viewed himself as a father figure to those who worked for him. "He went to funerals. He went to weddings. He went to bar mitzvahs," said Boyd. "Anybody who sent him an invitation to something at least heard back from him, even if he couldn't make a personal appearance."

In the company's early days, McGovern insisted on being one of the gang. When an IDC analyst was moving into a new house on a Saturday, McGovern showed up with a bucket of Kentucky Fried Chicken, ready to help carry furniture or paint walls. "Come on," he said, "I'll help you move in."

Over the decades, McGovern had a cast of administrative assistants and secretaries who supported his insane travel schedule and facilitated his connections to his people. Dolaher, who joined IDG as a receptionist after a short-lived stint as road manager for Aerosmith (she couldn't tolerate the wild, drug-filled environment), began work as McGovern's executive assistant in 1983. She started work on a Monday, and by that Thursday, McGovern came to her and said, "We need to go to China." IDG was in the process of setting up its nascent China operations, and McGovern was making an increasing number of trips to Beijing. "It would be really good if you could come and help me," he said to an astonished Dolaher, who had not only never been out of the country but had never flown on a plane.

Dolaher flew by herself to Beijing, a city that in those days retained all the vestiges of the Mao-era communist regime. It was just beginning to embrace a global market economy. When she arrived at the airport, she had no idea where to go and with whom to speak. The airport was crawling with soldiers carrying automatic weapons, and as she approached customs, there on the other side of the barrier were Pat and his wife, Lore. Dolaher breathed a sigh of relief and embarked on a whirlwind experience as McGovern wined and dined Chinese government officials, ministers, and other key constituents in his effort to set up a publishing company.

Beyond the successful China business venture, Dolaher knew that McGovern took special pride in knowing that he had given many people careers they wouldn't otherwise have had. He developed an educational program for employees to help get them up to speed about publishing, and the government took part in everything. "It was an era when *nobody* was being welcomed into China, and IDG was," she said. "And it was really because of Pat's personality and his drive and his ability to negotiate. He knew how to get to yes."

As he became more and more focused on IDG's growing venture capital business, McGovern brought his innate sensibility to those encounters. Unlike employees, who had intrinsic reasons to be in awe of their boss, the entrepreneurs in whom IDG invested were an independent and iconoclastic lot. They were seeking a path to a successful enterprise, and investors were often seen as necessary evils, money folks who were taking a significant piece of ownership of a fledgling enterprise in exchange for capital and insight.

In China, where venture capital investing has only soared since the late 1990s, the Silicon Valley model wasn't always the best way to approach Chinese entrepreneurs. Jim Breyer, who formed a partnership with IDG Capital in China, met many times with McGovern and the entrepreneurs with whom they'd invested. McGovern, Breyer said, was always positive, always encouraging, while Breyer tended to be more impatient about the progress a new venture was making.

"I would often be the one to say, 'We're off our one-year plan. What do we do to get back on track to meet product development goals?' Pat would rarely be focused on that set of milestones," Breyer said. "Rather, he would be very encouraging to the entrepreneurs and the team about the progress they were making and how fundamentally interesting this could be long term."

In considering business folklore, it is far easier to identify iconoclastic leaders who ruled with a heavy hand. But Pat McGovern thought and acted otherwise. Henry David Thoreau once said, "If a man does not keep pace with his companions, perhaps it is because he hears a different drummer. Let him step to the music which he hears, however measured or far away."

In the annals of business history, most successful CEOs have been capable of hearing a drumbeat, spotting the parade, and jumping out in front of it. There is nothing inherently wrong with this tactic, and indeed, business acumen dictates that this is a laudable leadership method. For McGovern, opportunity was all about gathering the trombones, the snare drums, and the trumpets, getting the skilled players to don the uniforms and pick up the instruments, and leading the parade. For 50 years, McGovern embodied Thoreau's words and stepped purposefully to his own music—music that was heard around the world.

"You don't encounter leaders like Pat very often," said Maryfran Johnson. "These are leaders people will follow from company to company. It's more than genuine charisma. He had a level of engagement you could not fake. He never needed to fake it because that's who he really was."

TAKEAWAYS

▶▶ Be willing to do almost anything to motivate the troops. People respond to genuine self-deprecation.

▶▶ An engaged and motivated workforce is cost-effective. It's worth the effort to make that engagement happen.

▶▶ Having people feel good about themselves is a powerful way to manage.

▶▶ Be the cheerleader for your company.

▶▶ Make sure employees share in the company's success, both financially and emotionally.

11

LESSON TEN
Love Your Employees,
Adore Your Customers

To succeed in business, you need to be
original, but you also need to understand
what your customers want.
—RICHARD BRANSON

If Pat McGovern had to narrow his leadership lessons to a single one, it would have been his deep belief in staying close to the customer. Indeed, the very motivation for founding IDG was based on his effort to find out what technology customers wanted and needed. His vision of a global technology revolution required a knowledgeable and informed user base that was well equipped to change the world. Everything flowed from that initial premise, and it became his muse and his guide for the next 50 years.

"We thought the most important thing to do would be to listen to customers and base your plans on the needs of the market," he said. With few exceptions, McGovern single-mindedly observed this dictate in everything he did at IDG. It was a foundational element that he shared with every executive and manager who worked for him over the decades, and it became the key corporate value that coursed through the veins of the organization.

"Pat taught us to focus, not on your competition, but on your customers," said IDC's Kirk Campbell. "He was always pushing us to meet with customers and come up with new products and services to meet their needs."

IDG managers, past and present, often repeated this mantra, and it was an invaluable lesson learned as they progressed in their own careers. Geography didn't matter; the continuous connection to customers had an impact in every corner of IDG's international empire.

For example, when Jim Casella was promoted from president of *InfoWorld* to chief operating office for all of IDG in 1994, he discovered a daunting aspect of his new assignment. In his new role, he was responsible for sending a personal note to each business unit head after each monthly review. If numbers were being met, the note would be short and congratulatory. If there were problems, and there were always problems in several markets, the missives had to be longer and more detailed. Given that there were more than 80 business units at the time, Casella found himself chained to his desk writing these notes instead of getting out to meet IDG customers as he'd planned.

After a couple of months of penning these notes, several of which had to address underperforming business units each month, he asked Pat McGovern for a meeting. The pair sat down in a small study next to McGovern's office in Boston, and Casella explained his plight.

"You know, Pat, I have to be honest with you. I'm finding this job a little challenging because you told me you really wanted me to get out and see customers and tell the IDG story," Casella said. "It's awfully hard to do that with 81 direct reports and everybody sending memos back and forth."

McGovern smiled and said, "Come here, I'm going to show you the secret of how to do this." They walked back into McGovern's office where he had an inbox on his desk overflowing with documents. It was material he was going to go over, dictate responses to his assistant, and address a raft of issues. He looked at Casella and said, "Let me show you how this works." He picked up the inbox, turned its contents upside down into the trash can. He said, "Anything that's really important, somebody will get back to you a second time and say, 'Hey, didn't you see what I sent you?'" He paused and added, "Go out and see IDG's customers and potential clients and don't worry about that." And that is what Casella did. "It was a pretty good lesson for me, that getting tied to a desk in a dynamic business wasn't what you wanted to do."

From McGovern, he learned an even bigger lesson. Building relationships with customers is not an effort that can be phoned in. You have to show up and be authentic and stay in touch. Casella, who eventually left IDG to start his own financial services company, continues to feel the power of that lesson. When visiting a prospective client for his new firm, he'll recall his IDG days, and ask, "When was the last time you met somebody in a senior management position from Thomson Reuters or Morningstar?" The client will think for a moment and usually reply, "I don't think I've ever met one of them." At which point Casella declares, "We really want your business and we really value the relationship, which is why I'm here. I really want to understand what we can do better, how we can continue to help you." The impact is substantial. "That really resonates with people," Casella said.

INVALUABLE ASSETS

McGovern was the ultimate road warrior. As much time as he spent with IDG employees, he spent twice that visiting customers. He didn't think of it as a burden but rather an essential encounter with measurable ROI.

In 1978, while driving back to Boston from New York, for example, McGovern decided to make an impromptu stop at

Turnkey Systems, a Norwalk, Connecticut–based software maker and *Computerworld* customer, both as advertiser and reader. At the reception desk in the lobby, he asked to speak to Lee Keet, the founder and president of Turnkey Systems, which made software used in the development of online transaction processing systems. McGovern had arrived without notice or an appointment and the receptionist, realizing that it was unusual for someone to drop in that way and ask for the head of the company, alerted Keet's administrative assistant.

Keet was in an executive committee meeting, and when his assistant slipped him a note that Patrick McGovern was waiting for him in the lobby, he quickly ended the meeting and greeted his surprise guest. They talked about the industry, about new software in the marketplace and IBM's troubling and aggressive position in that market, especially for a young software company trying to gain a foothold. They talked about IDG's new ventures in Europe and other countries. McGovern was not there to sell ads but to build a relationship. With a handshake, he left and headed home.

Keet was astonished by McGovern's visit and how dedicated he was to staying close to customers and listening attentively to them. Unannounced visits from media publishers were unheard of, and it was the kind of encounter that remained vivid for Keet, even decades later.

Every CEO *claims* that his company is laser-focused on the customer. It has become a mantra and a cliché. But in every industry, from the airlines to banking, those words often come up empty and meaningless. Anyone who has tried to squeeze their average-size body into a modern airline seat, for example, realizes immediately that the airlines regard their customers as merely statistics in an algorithm aimed at maximizing profits. McGovern viewed his customers as invaluable assets, and it had a major impact on IDG's growth and profitability. He knew his customers, offered them what they wanted, showed them what they needed, and learned from them and with them. As IDG's influence grew, this leadership trait got kudos from key industry players.

Jeff Bezos, founder and CEO of Amazon, said, "I think IDG has a good product in part because they work hard in a fairly structured and disciplined way to stay on top of the market and try to figure out what customers want."[1]

"The publications that IDG produces are really a vital link between the industry and customers," added Michael Dell of Dell Computers.[2]

McGovern was responsible for this structured and disciplined connection to customers. His visit to Keet was simply standard procedure for McGovern. He made a point of regularly taking important clients out to lunch or dinner to get to know them better. He actually enjoyed accompanying IDG sales reps on sales calls so he could stay close to them and their business needs. And he encouraged key customers to join him and the company's managers at IDG off-site meetings and planning sessions to ensure that the customer perspective was fully represented in strategy planning.

"Pat always felt that all customers had important stories to tell, and he was always eager to listen to them," said Steve Woit, a former IDG executive and publisher. "He treated them as individuals and encouraged his people to try to figure out ways to meet their needs and make them successful. He felt that if we made our customers successful, we would be successful as well."

To that end, McGovern compulsively went on customer sales calls for almost his entire run at IDG. He would either go alone, as he had done with Keet, or with IDG publishers and sales executives. Who accompanied him was less important than the environment he encountered at each visit. He was not interested in a simple handshake, a cup of coffee, and a quick exit. He wanted to hear firsthand what the customer's business goals were and to understand their products, to hear their thoughts about the IDG products they used, and to converse at a very senior level about IT and economic and political trends. He often heard the suggestion that he run for political office someday, a path for which he had little interest.

From the beginning, McGovern had a unique ability to see opportunities that others were missing. *Computerworld* emerged as the highly profitable bible of the industry because McGovern took a different approach to trade publishing. Most trade journals circulate within the industry sector they serve. *Computerworld* instead served a profession, once known as electronic data processing (EDP) which later morphed into information technology. EDP experts could be found across industries. The data processing manager of an insurance company, though in a different industry than his counterpart at a manufacturing company, was a kindred spirit. They didn't compete with each other, but they all needed *Computerworld* to understand the trends and news of the computer industry and how it would impact their companies. It was a powerful sales tool.

"*Computerworld*'s approach to its advertisers was the most consultative," said Jack Edmonston, who was *Computerworld*'s marketing director during the 1970s and early 1980s. "We offered data on their customers, and provided free research on their products and services using *Computerworld* subscribers. We even helped them produce better advertising."

As a neophyte publishing company CEO, McGovern soon had a tiger by the tail as revenues soared, and he set his sights on a simple but effective tactic: please the customers so much they will sell the product for you. The concept worked across IDG's ever-expanding line of publications.

Over a 20-year span, Pat Kenealy accompanied McGovern on well over a hundred sales calls. The pair visited everyone from junior media buyers at small agencies to chief marketing officers. They met budding entrepreneurs and established industry giants like Ken Olsen, Bill Gates, Larry Ellison, John Chambers, Jim Barksdale, and Eric Schmidt. "Pat visited Michael Dell when Dell was small, and he visited when Dell was huge," Kenealy said. He also made stops at all the major IT firms such as IBM and Hewlett-Packard.

Many of these famous players weren't sure what to make of McGovern until they got a firsthand taste of his technical sophistication, his understanding of the diverse and complex technology landscape and the attendant markets. His routine was consistent, whether he was meeting with the rich and famous or the less well known.

According to Kenealy, an IDG business unit manager would receive a call from McGovern's assistant saying that "Pat would like to spend some time with customers." The answer was always yes, and not just because the request came from the boss. Because of his stature in the industry, McGovern's presence opened every door, including those who had resisted earlier entreaties from IDG salespeople.

His office would request three or four sales calls in a day over breakfasts, lunches, and dinners, along with a full account briefing for each prospective client meeting. These had to arrive a week in advance so McGovern could read them. The publisher or sales rep would pick up McGovern at his hotel, the airport, or his home, and if he hadn't already read the briefing, he would do so on the ride to the client. "Either way, he had it memorized verbatim by the time we got to the first customer," Kenealy said.

Accompanying McGovern was not for the faint of heart. His incomparable stamina shamed people half his age, and he was renowned for his rare but memorable bouts of impatience. Kenealy recalled riding with McGovern and a veteran IDG sales rep in Southern California on a long day of sales calls. McGovern, having clearly gotten up on the wrong side of the bed, spent the drive reading directions from a map for a "better route" to the customer site and debating every turn the sales rep wanted to make. That she lived in the area mattered little to him. His surly mood disappeared as he walked, calm and smiling, into the meeting armed with everything he had read on the tip of his tongue. Satisfied after the meeting, he congratulated the sales rep on "her excellent knowledge of the territory," and told her that she had taught him some new shortcuts as well as valuable ideas in the meeting.

Even as he got older, McGovern was in constant motion. On a venture capital trip to the United Kingdom in 2001, McGovern alerted the IDG Europe venture capital team that he'd be visiting, along with Kenealy, and he wanted to call on some portfolio companies. He flew from Boston on a red-eye flight, landed in London where he met Kenealy, and the IDG team loaded the pair into a van. They proceeded to visit eight portfolio companies and a small cadre of entrepreneurs from London to Oxford and back to London. Operating on little sleep, it was a long, grueling day.

"He performed unbelievably," Kenealy said. "He knew as deeply as you could rationally expect the technology of these really disparate companies." Each visit went longer than scheduled. The day grew longer as the group arrived later and later for each successive appointment. The final meeting was a dinner in Piccadilly in London. As they were driving toward the city, Kenealy turned around and there was McGovern, fast asleep, his huge body wedged between two venture capitalists, on their way to the eighth appointment. But he awoke, slightly refreshed, and happily attended the dinner.

"How many chairmen would do that?" Kenealy thought to himself. After the dinner, they went back to the hotel, and the group loudly declined an invitation from McGovern to keep the party going. "He had run the natives, who had ten hours of sleep the night before and two weeks getting ready for his visit, into the ground," Kenealy said. "Anyone else would have said, 'Let's skip the last one,' " but he just went with it."

BELIEVE THE SURVEYS

McGovern was also a ubiquitous presence at countless trade shows, both IDG's own events and others, where he would wander the aisles, stopping to speak with countless exhibitors and attendees. McGovern was a fixture in the front row of every Macworld Expo, greeting attendees, taking endless notes, and staying for the entire event. He knew his presence was more than a plug for the show. It was a statement to customers that their needs and concerns were deeply important to him. If there was a chance to learn something new, he was always game. If he could promote IDG's brand along the way, so much the better.

As a regular visitor to the annual CEBIT show, the world's largest IT fair, in Hannover, Germany, McGovern spent days moving through the cavernous halls, visiting vendor booths and scoping out the industry's future. At CEBIT, IDG Germany sponsored a big customer meeting and dinner each year at a village outside the city. According to York von Heimburg, the traffic in Hannover during CEBIT was so snarled that the company arranged a helicopter to fly customers to the dinner. When McGovern's assistant heard about the helicopter, she warned von Heimburg about McGovern's fear of small planes and helicopters. For a customer encounter, McGovern overcame his panic, climbed into the helicopter, and made a graceful entrance for dinner.

McGovern was fanatical about reaching out to readers and advertisers to hear what they thought about IDG's family of publications. He insisted that every operating unit contract with third-party firms to send out regular customer satisfaction surveys, which he often reviewed personally. He took these surveys seriously and made significant changes based on what trends emerged from the responses. The surveys were the basis of a guidance mechanism for all of IDG. Bonuses were earned, new products launched, careers made or broken.

"If we see that the customers are getting less satisfied, that we are no longer number one, then we'll feed back the result, and we'll ask the manager what steps they are taking to fix that," McGovern said.

He liked to point out that this kind of feedback taught him *the importance of having customers on the board of directors of the company.* "If you listen to what people want and respond, then you do very well," he said. "If you try to dream up what you'd like to do and try to force it into the marketplace, then you are going to have much higher risks and you won't be successful because you're not responding to other people's needs."

When he began to build an international company, he insisted on hiring local managers because they were closer to the customers and knew what those customers wanted. Nothing seemed more obnoxious to him than the assumption that a centralized authority, thousands of miles away in Boston, knew what IT readers in Munich, Tokyo, Beijing, or Buenos Aires wanted.

Unlike many corporate leaders, McGovern asked for advice and actually took the advice from people he believed knew what they were doing. He sought wisdom not only from his managers and employees but from customers, suppliers, even job applicants, and he listened deeply to what they had to say. He could be mulishly stubborn when it came to defending and supporting his beloved publications around the world, but he never dismissed valuable customer feedback.

"He had some quite basic principles that really applied," said Kit Gould, the UK country manager. "One of the things that really struck me was that he always put the customer, the reader, the visitor to our sites, the delegates at conferences, at the forefront of everyone's mind. Because if you had that, and you had the trust and relationship with those customers, that led to an unending and constant conversation. He was very focused on circulation and traffic growth and pricing, and he focused *you* on that, which was a really good thing."

Gould acknowledged that IDG had a rough time for many years trying to crack the UK market. But when it finally did, IDG significantly outperformed competitors such as Ziff Davis, CMP, and other rivals. "The reason they didn't win and IDG won and came out stronger and better for it was because we put the readers first, not the advertisers," Gould said.

Given the dynamics of information technology during McGovern's reign at IDG, the task of effectively connecting with audiences in the United States and around the world was daunting, to say the least. Few industries went through as many tectonic shifts as information technology, and staying ahead of the trends required focused effort and smart employees. Dictates from IDG's

Boston headquarters could never supplant the viral spread of McGovern's ideas about leadership and about meeting customers' needs regardless of geography. In 1998, IDG published a sales brochure replete with postage-stamp-sized covers of each of the company's 295 publications. It was a company tradition to periodically send out this brochure, which had begun as a one-pager back in the early 1970s. Now, unfolded, the eight-page brochure measured over five feet long, and bespoke the breadth and reach of the massive company. It was impressive for IDG's 90 million technology buyers (readers who made corporate buying decisions) in 75 countries and illustrated the payoff for customer intimacy.

IDG editors around the globe polled readers, often doing research ahead of designing an issue. It wasn't out of the ordinary for these publications to offer readers five different subjects from which to choose as a cover story and a headline, or to incorporate their input into special issues and new areas of coverage. Every customer, therefore, was a potential resource in McGovern's quest to build IDG into the world's leading purveyor of information about information technology.

Gould recalled a European managers meeting in London in which a team-building scavenger hunt was organized. The exercise, meant to be fun and accompanied by some serious beer-drinking, required teams to travel around London looking for various items on the scavenger hunt list. Gould was on McGovern's team, along with York von Heimburg from IDG Germany, and they found themselves on the London Underground, traveling to one of the designated locations.

In the subway car, McGovern noticed three different riders reading IDG's *PC Advisor* magazine. "You've planted these people," von Heimburg complained to Gould. "Honest to God, I haven't," Gould protested, though thrilled by the serendipitous encounter with one of his publications.

McGovern didn't hesitate. He went over to one of the readers and began asking questions. "Why are you reading that publication? Why did you buy that one? What do you like about it?" He didn't reveal that he owned the company that published the magazine. "He was delighted, and I know that even a great PR firm couldn't have set that up," said Gould. "He expected the world to be full of his magazines because technology was the cornerstone of everything. He spotted that way before anyone else, that it was the driving force."

Conversations with readers offered game-changing ideas. For example, when McGovern began to publish *Computerworld* in 1967, he believed readers longed for a publication that was on their side and would speak as an advocate for the customers in the tech industry. "At the end of one day of interviewing in New York, we kept getting a message that people want something, a publication that reports on what they're doing, that builds a community among the people who head up data centers," McGovern recalled. "They wanted it frequently, and apparently, they were willing to pay a subscription fee for it. So that sounded like a business opportunity." And *Computerworld* was born.

Ted Bloom, who began working for McGovern as a high school student in Newton, Massachusetts, in the 1960s, rose to the post of CFO and president over his decades with IDG. He pointed out that McGovern had three simple circles of business that he followed unwaveringly:

1. Stay close to your customer. Do readership surveys so you know what your readers want.
2. Meet your financial goals without requiring debt or a public offering.
3. Stay close to your assets. Always measure how your employees feel and how things are progressing.

"We didn't buy printing presses or paper mills," Bloom said. "We always outsourced things that were capital intensive to allow us to develop editorial staff and new products."

LEADING FROM THE FRONT

As executives came and went, McGovern's obsession with the company's customers was passed like a virus to everyone in a leadership role. Bob Carrigan, who spent eight years as CEO of IDG Communications, was always aware of McGovern's preoccupation with customer satisfaction. "The technology media category, by definition, included some of the fastest-moving companies on the planet. As such, it was an imperative to stay close—more so than perhaps most other media categories," said Carrigan.

As Carrigan pointed out, many new IDG products and publications such as *CIO* magazine and *Network World*, were launched because of customer feedback and keeping a close watch on the market. "Tech marketers were among the most experimental of all marketers," Carrigan added, "so if you wanted to do an effective job in meeting their needs, again, you had to stay especially close."

He noted how McGovern was among the first publishing industry leaders to acknowledge the shift from print to digital. "Tech marketers were among the first to shift large ad budgets to digital," Carrigan said.

By paying close attention to customer yearnings and being able to catch on early to the inevitable power of the Internet, McGovern broke the once-sacred publishing industry bonds with print. Around the turn of the millennium, publishers were reluctant to shift to or add online versions of their content, but McGovern pushed forward into this uncharted territory. It was and remains a painful transition for newspapers and magazines, which have had to forge new revenue streams to replace vast lost income from the decline of advertising sales. Many didn't survive.

In a 2008 *New York Times* article, IDG was credited with being at the forefront of the inevitable transfer from print to digital. "The excellent thing, and good news, for publishers is that there is life after print—in fact, a better life after print," McGovern said in the article.

IDG was among the first publishing companies to shift its revenue stream from print to digital. By 2008, 52 percent of its ad sales came from online rather than print. McGovern told the *New York Times* that IDG not only had made the transformation but that the company was experiencing 10 percent annual growth, even with this tectonic shift.[3] But the Great Recession that began at the end of 2008 hit IDG hard, as it did every other publisher, and this achievement was obscured by the sudden battle for survival in the media business. It was a difficult time for IDG around the world.

It was around this time that McGovern began experiencing health problems, but he refused to slow down. Troubled economic times required more, not less effort. Carrigan accompanied McGovern on countless customer visits. "He studied the people he was meeting with to an almost uncomfortable level," Carrigan said. "He knew so much about them. He learned everything about them that he could."

At these meetings, McGovern had barely taken his seat when he would commence unveiling his knowledge of the customer's company and career. "Oh, I see that from 1992 to 1994, you were in the National Guard" or some other personal anecdote he'd discovered. He was apt to go through a person's entire history. "He did that to show humility," Carrigan said, "and to connect with people and show that he cared enough. The customer would be like, 'Oh my God, this billionaire just recited my whole history.' People were always blown away by it."

Carrigan recalled that McGovern's main source of client contact was through conferences and events. He never missed an IDG event where large pools of customers gathered. At some, McGovern would give an inspirational welcome speech, "but his real impact was sitting in the audience, usually in the front row, throughout the entire event, mingling with customers," Carrigan said. Such presence had an impact on IDG employees who witnessed their chairman's routine. "It just reinforced the things that Pat always said about being in the market with customers all the time. In other words, if he could be there listening and engaging, so should you."

Ultimately, the common thread in these stories is the consistency McGovern displayed in his relentless embrace of his customers, a pattern of behavior that has served IDG well since its founding. "There are a million such stories," Pat Kenealy said, "but the moral of them all is to be prepared, be passionate about your customers' products and business, and treat everyone as important, from the assistant media buyer to the CEOs.

"Pat led from the front with customers," he continued. "It gave him the unfiltered truth about what customers were doing, thinking, and planning. I learned something on every customer visit with him. For 20 years, when I was with him on the road, he was mythically good, and for 20 years before that, people tell me he was the same."

For young entrepreneurs seeking inspiration, McGovern demonstrated that there is no substitute for embracing your enterprise beyond all else. He loved information technology and IT entrepreneurs, and he was passionate about the impact IT had on the world. IDG's customers had a visceral sense of the man's enthusiasm because he openly shared it with the world. Nearly 50 years after he began, he was as enamored of his mission as he had ever been, and work was the fuel for the mission. "Pat loved interesting people," said John Gallant, a veteran IDG editor. "A lot of folks on the business side didn't have as much interest in the industry, but Pat was deeply involved and engaged in it." He was, Gallant observed, "completely attentive to whatever he was doing."

Such devotion can't be faked or forced, and the technology roadside is littered with the remnants of start-ups whose founders aimed at a quick hit and a fast exit. McGovern succeeded beyond all expectations not only because he loved what he did completely and stayed the course, but because he understood that success lay at the end of a journey where you focused, not on the competition, but on your customers.

TAKEAWAYS

▶▶ Listen to customers and base your plans on the needs of the market.

▶▶ Spend as much time as possible with customers. It has measurable ROI.

▶▶ Accompany sales reps on customer calls and pay attention as they share business goals.

▶▶ Take every customer meeting; don't let fatigue end the day early.

▶▶ Put customers on your board of directors. Be guided by them.

▶▶ Do customer surveys and act on the results.

12

FORWARD,
ALWAYS FORWARD

*If you would not be forgotten as soon as
you are dead, either write something worth
reading or do something worth writing.*
—BENJAMIN FRANKLIN

When Hugo Shong, the global chairman of IDG Capital in China, stepped to the microphone, he quickly became choked up with emotion. Shong stood before a small crowd of invited guests at the McGovern Institute for Brain Research at MIT on an unusually mild January evening in 2017. He was there to celebrate the acquisition of IDG by a consortium of IDG Capital, Shong's Beijing-based venture capital firm, and China Oceanwide Holdings Group, a major Chinese business conglomerate. Pat McGovern had died nearly three years earlier, and his passing triggered a protracted and sometimes painful process of finding a future for IDG.

It was a bittersweet moment for most of the attendees because it marked the official end of an era, a passing of a torch that had remained lit since 1964, when McGovern had founded his remarkable company in a small gray house in Newton, Massachusetts.

The institute's splendid atrium, with its breathtaking golden brain sculpture by artist Ralph Helmick, was filled with IDG executives, board members, and a group from China Oceanwide, all on hand to honor a noteworthy past and the expectations of a promising but uncertain future. Helmick's sculpture, which had been donated by Shong, was composed of 100 bronze and stainless steel "neurons," and viewed from the atrium, formed the shape of a human brain. At the same time, it had the feel of a globe, stretching out unevenly but inevitably in all directions, as IDG had under McGovern's long and extraordinary tenure.

Among the attendees that night were Lore Harp McGovern, Pat's wife; his two children from his first marriage, Patrick III and Elizabeth, representing the The Patrick J. McGovern Foundation; Robert Desimone, director of the Brain Institute; and Walter Boyd, IDG's chairman and McGovern's loyal associate for a half-century. All were deeply moved by the occasion, but it was especially poignant for Shong, who had learned much of what he knew about business and leadership from McGovern. It was McGovern who had brought him into IDG 22 years earlier and taught him the business so that he could lead IDG's pioneering efforts in China. Two days before McGovern died on March 19, 2014, Shong had been at his bedside to say farewell, and now, nearly three years later, he still felt the loss profoundly. He'd often told colleagues that McGovern was like a father to him.

Wearing one of McGovern's signature yellow ties with a dark business suit, Shong told the gathering that he had chosen this MIT location for the official announcement of the long-awaited deal because he knew how much the Brain Institute meant to McGovern. In order to continue funding the Institute, the Foundation had to arrange the sale of the company. At the podium, he affirmed his commitment to keep IDG alive and thriving despite the change in ownership.

He recounted how he had spoken to the gravely ill McGovern in the hospital. "I said to him, 'Pat, you created two legacies,'"

McGovern with Hugo Shong in Beijing.

Shong told the gathering as his voice broke. " 'One is IDG and the other is the Brain Institute.' I promised him that I would keep those two legacies alive for years to come. This process for me is not about business. It is really to fulfill the promise I made before Pat passed away. I know he would be happy to see it all come together." Breaking into tears, Shong took a moment and added, "His spirit is here. I will say what Pat always said: 'The best is yet to come.' "

A PROPHET FOR HIS AGE

Legacies can be fragile structures. The more accomplished an individual, the more scrutiny gets focused on that person's achievements. Few could find fault with McGovern's achievements. His death in 2014 at age 76, after a long, unpublicized battle with heart disease, stunned the industry and left IDG employees, especially longtime veterans, grieving the loss of this singular individual who touched so many lives. McGovern, who believed himself indestructible and never considered retiring, had a rarely matched 50-year tenure atop a global corporation. There were questionable decisions and inevitable failures along the way, but the result of his leadership was steady growth, visionary ideas, and an uncanny ability to hire talented people, hear their stories, and allow them to build onto the greater structure of the company. His faith in people to take their ideas and harvest profitable ventures paid significant dividends both in the United States and across international borders.

"He was a sharp, considerate, and astute leader," said Kumaran Ramanathan, an IDG veteran who became the president of IDG Communications after the sale of the company. "He had the aura of greatness around him, but at the same time, he never traded on that. His passing hit us all in so many ways. There were a lot of tears shed."

Business stories rarely have fairy-tale endings. When a wealthy, widely influential leader dies, the event ripples outward to every corner of an organization and beyond, and often brings unexpected turmoil and tribulation. Grief does not usually mix well with financial challenges.

Upon his death, the company he loved was suddenly cast into an unsettling quandary. Given that he had never thought about retirement and had continued to serve as IDG's vibrant guiding spirit, McGovern's death was especially earthshaking. He had kept his illness under wraps in the belief that he would recover and get back to his life's work. Few inside IDG were prepared for the news that he was gone.

How would the company go forward without its founder, chairman, and muse? Who would take over the reins? How could anyone else replace a man who had not only built the company from scratch but infused it over a half-century with his essential tenets of life, commerce, fierce dedication to his corporate values, and the unceasing desire to keep it moving forward?

Such tectonic shifts for an organization are usually followed by periods of uncertainty, as the stakeholders try to create and jump-start a new vision for the future. The status quo rarely holds, and upheaval arrives like an unwanted guest for many executives and employees. But this cannot erase the indelible achievements and timeless lessons in leadership that McGovern left behind. In fact, his legacy, which is multilayered and diverse, is firmly intact.

China Oceanwide is now the majority owner of IDG. Given the complex nature of the media business in the Internet age, new strategies and ideas will shape the company's future.

It is fitting, in many ways, that the company was acquired by a Chinese organization because McGovern's unprecedented foray into China, starting in 1980, is a noteworthy facet of his legacy. Indeed, IDG's global reach bespeaks his influence in nearly 100 countries around the world. He accomplished his goal of spreading knowledge about information technology to developing markets, hungry for news about this brewing revolution. But the remarkable success of IDG in China, in both media and venture capital, fueled by McGovern's vision and willingness to move into such uncharted territory, has been an indelible part of nearly all remembrances of the man's life work.

"He's totally revered there," said George Colony, founder and chairman of Forrester Research. "How many US business leaders have translated their expertise to another culture and found that culture actually believed in it and accepted it? That's amazing. That might be his greatest legacy."

When asked, in a 2000 video interview with Daniel Morrow, executive director of *Computerworld*'s Honors Program, about how he wanted to be remembered, McGovern was clear but characteristically humble.

"I hope that I could be remembered as contributing to the process that led to so many wonderful advances in the quality of life because of the development of computers and communications and electronics," he said. He hoped that people would connect this achievement with "the flow of timely and accurate, and provocative and stimulating information" offered by IDG's publications and research. The mission was to inform and educate a global audience about where technology was and where it could and would be in the future. "I just hope that people will judge that the process IDG created has accelerated the benefits of this technology for the benefit of future generations," he added.

In fact, McGovern appears to have brilliantly orchestrated the very legacy he deeply desired. He was aware, over at least a decade before his death, that IDG faced big challenges in the tumultuous technology media world. He had spearheaded the shift from print to digital earlier than most publishers and understood the perils of seeking profitable growth in this new environment. Given how technology itself changes with lightning speed and how businesses and individuals quickly adapt to these changes, the old rules no longer applied. Though he never wavered in his devotion to his original core business, he began to focus his attention on venture capital, neuroscience research, and new ways to perpetuate his mission.

McGovern directed nearly 100 percent of his net worth into the newly established Patrick J. McGovern Foundation, which was fully funded in 2017 with $1.3 billion from the sale of IDG. The Foundation is now poised to become a formidable force in funding research in the fields of information technology and neuroscience, the crown jewels in McGovern's two profoundly heartfelt missions. They may seem like disparate disciplines, but for McGovern, the intersection of information technology and neuroscience was at the heart of his lifelong dream. The ability to understand and radically impact the human brain was only going to be made possible with the advent of the most advanced technology.

The McGovern Institute for Brain Research is now among the world's leading neuroscience research facilities, with world-class faculty pursuing Nobel Prize–quality efforts. For example, McGovern researchers Feng Zhang and Ed Boyden have made breakthrough discoveries in molecular biology, genetics, and neuroscience and are widely considered among the most transformative scientists of their generation. Zhang discovered how to edit the genomes of living things, including humans, using a tool called CRISPR. This tool, which Zhang has made widely available, has the potential to treat some of the greatest causes of human suffering, from brain disorders to cancer to blindness. As graduate students at Stanford, Zhang and Boyden developed a technology to control brain activity with light. Optogenetics, as it is called, reveals the circuits of the brain in exquisite detail and has accelerated biomedical research worldwide. Boyden developed an audacious imaging technique called expansion microscopy in which brain tissue is expanded up to 100 times its original volume, making brain circuits easier to see with conventional microscopes.

As he devoted his time to the neuroscience effort, McGovern had also become deeply involved in IDG's venture capital funds in the United States, China, and other countries. Having set these firms in motion in the 1990s and early 2000s, the venture funds have weathered the dot-com meltdown and a devastating global recession in 2008 to emerge stronger than ever. IDG venture funds around the world now manage more than $3.6 billion in technology investments. McGovern reveled in not only the lucrative financial returns from these prescient technology investments but in his ability to support talented young entrepreneurs. Throughout his five decades with IDG, he never lost the entrepreneurial zeal he experienced in the early days of his own start-up. He encouraged entrepreneurial behavior within IDG and loved meeting and mentoring founders, from Silicon Valley to Bangalore.

McGovern never looked back. IDG's future was forward and that was where he relentlessly went. People who knew him well described McGovern as the business world's best cheerleader, a leader content to urge others toward success. Nearly everyone he met noted his total recall for names, dates, and events and for his intuitive sense of people. Hourlong job interviews often turned into half-day-long encounters, not only because he wanted to make good hiring choices but because he was insatiably curious about what he could learn from other smart people. He was affable, playful, and verbose at times. Although he was deeply private about his personal life, he was unabashed in promoting his company and his people above himself.

He made IDG his mission and his mantra. He stayed relent-lessly close to IDG's customers, fostered a family atmosphere for the company's tens of thousands of employees, kept his finger on the financial pulse of the company, and had an uncanny knack for identifying vibrant potential markets. He embraced risk, and he gave people the means and support to try new ideas. He praised success but graciously accepted failure. And he circled the globe time and again, flying 300,000 miles each year, to stay closely connected to his empire. "Maybe a quarter or a fifth of the publications he launched died along the way," said Pat Kenealy. "He didn't bat a thousand, but he batted well over .500, and he had the courage to keep going up to bat."

McGovern's leadership traits, taken individually, were not unique. Other corporate leaders have impressive credentials and notable character attributes. What is notable, however, is that while other prominent leaders may have exhibited two or three of McGovern's traits, few had all of them. He did it all, and most astonishing was his ability to consistently and tirelessly apply those traits for his entire tenure as IDG's chairman. The idea that he was able to do things, more or less the same way, for all that time was the key to his success. That doesn't mean he was intractable or stuck in the past. On the contrary, he navigated the countless tectonic shifts in the technology landscape and never missed a beat. He was firm in his beliefs but flexible in his ability to embrace new market trends and workplace realities. Like few other leaders, his work ethic and strength of character matched his intellect and business acumen. In that regard, he was essentially the same leader at the end of his career as he had been at the outset. As his health deteriorated, he simply refused to slow down.

"You would tell him not to come to the board meetings," Kenealy said. "But he insisted on doing what he always did."

Given the scope of his empire and his unusual longevity in a leadership role, the lessons he offered numbered well beyond the

10 upon which this book has focused. Because he made it his business to reach out and connect with as many of the tens of thousands of IDG employees, advertisers, and readers around the world as he possibly could, every individual encounter likely left an indelible personal lesson. But these 10 offer a broad foundation for what McGovern spent his career implanting in his organization:

- Forge a mission that matters, and let your people know you are on the mission together.

- Embrace the road less traveled and chart a path along that road.

- Hire the warriors, empower them, and nurture their talent and you will win.

- Encourage entrepreneurial behavior and back it up with a sincere "Let's try it" attitude.

- Optimism is infectious. Always remind the troops that "The best is yet to come!"

- Build a decentralized organization because when creating a global empire, every market is local.

- Integrity is a priceless characteristic of a brand, so never cross that line in the sand.

- "Loose-tight" leadership is an effective way to build a huge, global organization. Letting every manager have nearly unlimited control is powerful, but never forget that someone has to have the final word and stand firm.

- Let the CEO be the chief encouragement officer, a relentless cheerleader who makes sure his employees feel the support and commitment.

- Love your employees, but adore your customers. Real customer focus beyond the lip service is challenging and time-consuming. But it always pays off.

McGovern is remembered by those who became part of his wide orbit as an indefatigable life force for his company and his people. His boundless energy was titanic and awe-inspiring for his managers and executives who tried to keep up.

According to Jeffrey Rayport, McGovern created a self-fulfilling prophecy through his unshakable faith in his people and his company. "I never saw him, even for a nanosecond, projecting anything but that unflappable optimism and unshakable belief that IDG would win, that his people would win, and that everything would come out well. He baked that into the DNA of the company."

Ultimately, Patrick McGovern's legacy, one born and nurtured over 50 years, a legacy of not only stunning financial and business success but of authenticity and kindness, of ceaseless curiosity, of personal and meaningful contact with as many stakeholders as possible, fueled by superhuman energy and relentless optimism—that is a legacy that will stand the test of time.

ACKNOWLEDGMENTS

Embarking on a book project is mostly an act of faith. The effort can only reach its desired conclusion with the help of a great many people, most of whom graciously offer their time and insight for the cause.

First and foremost, my heartfelt thanks to Patrick J. McGovern III, who proposed this book project to me, and whose support, guidance, and friendship through this entire process made it a joyful and rewarding experience. He is, in all the best ways, his father's son.

Investigating the life and wisdom of Patrick McGovern for more than a year, I interviewed dozens of current and former IDG executives and employees, and each brought a personal and vital point of view of the man, the company, and the experience of being in McGovern's world. Without their stories and insight, this book couldn't have been written. I'm deeply grateful to all those who helped make this project a success.

My deep gratitude also goes to Walter Boyd, Pat Kenealy, Hugo Shong, and Sudhir Sethi for leading the way and providing not only memories but insightful analysis about Pat McGovern and what accounted for his remarkable achievements.

Many thanks to James Levine, the extraordinary literary agent from Levine/Greenberg/Rostan Literary Agency, for his guidance and support in making this book a reality. Thanks also to Casey Ebro, my superlative editor at McGraw-Hill, for taking a tall pile of pages and turning it into an actual book.

Of the many who provided invaluable insight and support along the way, special thanks go to George Harrar, Harry McCracken, Patricia Smith, Karen Ren, Raghunatha Rao, Mitch

Betts, Elizabeth McGovern, Raquel McGovern, Susan Odell, and Dan Farber at Salesforce.com.

A special group hug for my wife, Janie, and my home team: Cameron, Laura, Ben, and Lucy. Thanks for being my gravity when I start floating away.

NOTES

CHAPTER 1

1. "Media Brands," IDG corporate website, https://www.idg.com /advertise-with-us/media-brands/.
2. Edmund Berkeley, *Giant Brains*, the first popular book on electronic computers, http://www.historyofinformation.com/expanded.php?id =864.
3. Edmund C. Berkeley bio, IEEE Computer Society website, http:// history.computer.org/pioneers/berkeley.html.
4. Glenn Rifkin, "Investing in Brains," *Briefings* magazine, Q2 2012, https://mcgovern.mit.edu/images/stories/briefings-mcgovern.pdf.

CHAPTER 2

1. John Yemma, "Publishing All the Computer News That's Fit to Print," *Christian Science Monitor*, June 6, 1988.
2. Albert Scardino, "Computer-Magazine Giant Thrives on Global Approach," *New York Times*, July 31, 1989.

CHAPTER 3

1. "Hub Students Now in Clear After Arrest on Russian Trip," *Boston Globe*, July 30, 1960.
2. Victor D. Lippit, "The Political Economy of China's Economic Reform," *Critical Asian Studies* 37, no. 3 (2005): 441–462.
3. Li Xiguang, "China's Paper Tiger Hails from Boston," *Washington Post*, November 9, 1995.
4. Patrick J. McGovern, "Deng's True Legacy," *New York Times*, March 1997.
5. Jeffrey Bussgang, *Mastering the VC Game: A Venture Insider Reveals How to Get from Start-up to IPO on Your Terms* (Penguin, 2010).

CHAPTER 4

1. Warren Buffett, Letter to the Shareholders of Berkshire Hathaway, Inc., 1979, http://www.berkshirehathaway.com/letters/1979.html.
2. William N. Thorndike, *The Outsiders: Eight Unconventional CEOs and Their Radically Rational Blueprint for Success* (Harvard Business Review Press, 2012), 23.
3. Stuart Elliott, "IBM to Transfer Advertising Work to Single Agency," *New York Times*, May 25, 1994.

CHAPTER 5

1. Warren Bennis and Patricia Ward Biederman, *Organizing Genius: The Secrets of Creative Collaboration* (Basic Books, 1997), 211.

CHAPTER 6

1. Andrew Ross Sorkin and David D. Kirkpatrick, "'For Dummies' Parent Company Is Reported Close to Sale," *New York Times*, August 13, 2001.
2. For Dummies Store website, http://www.dummies.com/store.

CHAPTER 7

1. Bert Jacobs, "Why Optimistic Leaders Build the Healthiest Companies," *Inc.*, August 11, 2014.
2. Michael J. de la Merced, "William B. Ziff, Jr., 76, Builder of Magazine Empire, Dies," *New York Times*, September 12, 2006.
3. Harry McCracken, "After 30 Years, Macworld Is No Longer a Magazine," *Fast Company*, September 10, 2014.

CHAPTER 8

1. Alan Alper, "Computer Associates' Size Worries Some," *Computerworld*, August 3, 1987.
2. Bro Uttal, "Behind the Fall of Steve Jobs," *Fortune*, August 5, 1985.
3. Connie Guglielmo, "A Steve Jobs Moment That Mattered: Macworld, August 1997," *Forbes*, October 7, 2012.

4. David S. Joachim, "A Nod to Journalistic Integrity Is Seen in an Editor's Return," *New York Times*, May 14, 2007.
5. Narasu Rebbapragada and Alan Stafford, "10 Things We Hate About Apple," *Macworld*, May 7, 2007.

CHAPTER 9

1. Kenneth N. Gilpin, "Harold S. Geneen, 87, Dies; Nurtured ITT," *New York Times*, November 23, 1997.

CHAPTER 10

1. Paul B. Carroll, "Computer Publications Help to Create Legend of Patrick McGovern," *Wall Street Journal*, April 6, 1987.
2. Ibid.
3. David Zielenziger, "IDG's McGovern Sees IPO," *Bloomberg News*, May 14, 1996.
4. John Yemma, "The Main Man for Information," *Boston Globe*, April 9, 2000.
5. Robert X. Cringely, "So Pat McGovern Comes into a Bar," Beta News, March 21, 2014.

CHAPTER 11

1. Bezos, Jeff. "Patrick J. McGovern and Norman Pearlstine to Receive Lifetime Achievement Awards from the Magazine Industry." Video. November 10, 2004.
2. Dell, Michael. "Patrick J. McGovern and Norman Pearlstine to Receive Lifetime Achievement Awards from the Magazine Industry." Video. November 10, 2004.
3. Steve Lohr, "Publisher Tested the Waters Online, Then Dove In," *New York Times*, May 5, 2008.

INDEX

Page numbers in italic refer to photos or accompanying captions. "PMG" refers to Patrick J. McGovern, Jr.

ABOUT THE AUTHOR

Glenn Rifkin is a veteran journalist and author who has been a contributing writer for the *New York Times* business section for nearly 30 years and has written extensively on business and leadership for dozens of publications, including the *Wall Street Journal, Boston Globe, Harvard Business Review, Forbes*, and *Fortune*. Rifkin has consulted with a variety of companies, such as Boston Consulting Group, Korn Ferry International, Mercer Consulting, WPP, HCL Technologies, and PriceWaterhouseCoopers. He has also worked with Harvard Business School on editorial projects. He is the coauthor of *Radical Marketing: From Harvard to Harley, Lessons from Ten That Broke the Rules and Made It Big, The Ultimate Entrepreneur: The Story of Ken Olsen and Digital Equipment Corporation, The CEO and the Monk: One Company's Journey to Profit and Purpose*, and *Thoreau's Backyard: Musings from a Small Town*.

In the 1980s, Rifkin was a senior editor at *Computerworld*, IDG's leading publication, where he got a firsthand introduction to Patrick McGovern's remarkable leadership capabilities.

Rifkin lives in Acton, Massachusetts, with his wife, Jane, and their dog, Lucy.